SOME VIEWS ON ROCK PAINTINGS IN THE CEDERBERG

by
Janette Deacon

In 1991, the Department of Environment Affairs allocated research funds to the author for a detailed survey of the rock paintings in the Cederberg and Groot Winterhoek Wilderness Areas so that a record of sites could be kept and management guidelines could be drawn up for Cape Nature Conservation and Museums. In collaboration with Stephen Townley Bassett, who was responsible for the field surveys and recording of the paintings, 90 sites were found in the Cederberg Wilderness Area and 7 were recorded in the Groot Winterhoek Wilderness Area.

An important by-product of the project was public education. This book summarizes the results of the survey and draws on information from other people and institutions who have worked in the Cederberg area in general. It is part of a long-term programme to increase public awareness of rock art and to promote conservation of this important aspect of our heritage. The book is not designed to guide readers to rock art sites, but to help those who discover rock paintings during hikes in the mountains, or during visits to sites that are open to the public, to gain a better understanding of what the paintings mean.

ISBN 1 875012 25 7

Published by the National Monuments Council, PO Box 4637, Cape Town, 8000

First published 1994
Second edition 1998

Design and Layout : Left Justified cc
Maps: Left Justified cc
Photographs: Janette Deacon: Cover and Figures 4, 5, 7, 8, 13, 17, 18, 19, 21, 23-31
Stephen Townley Bassett: Figures 3, 10, 11, 12, 14, 20
Tracings: Janette Deacon: p. 53
Stephen Townley Bassett: Cover and pp. (i), 1-6, 8-10, 13, 16-19, 21-23, 27, 29-32, 34-35, 37-38, 44, 50-51, 62
The Spatial Archaeology Research Unit at the University of Cape Town: p. 43

Repro by Castle Graphics
Printed by ABC Press, 24 Kinghall Avenue, Epping

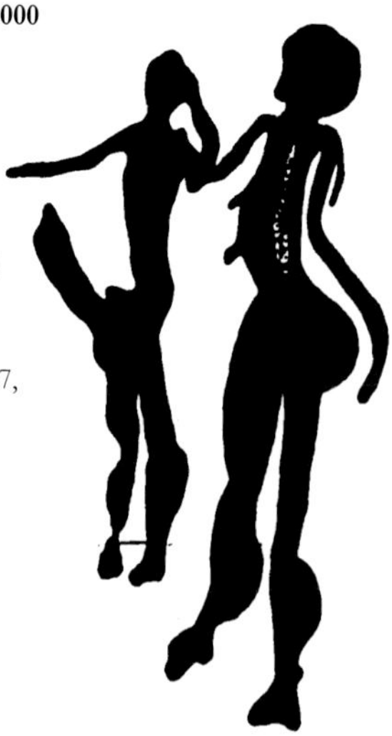

CONTENTS

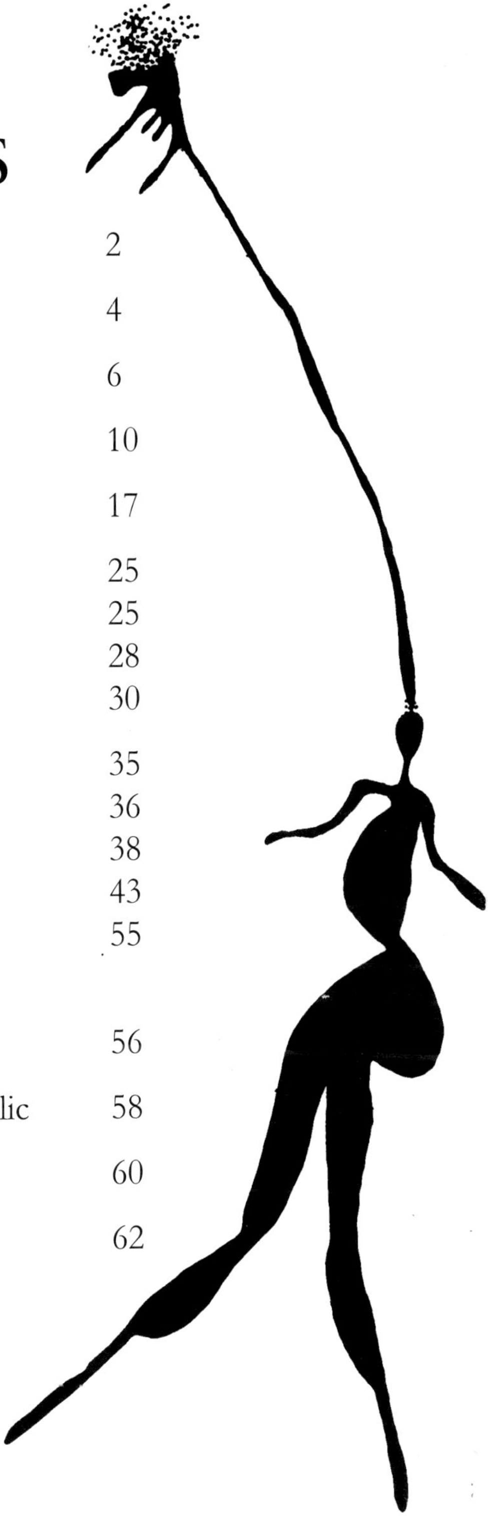

ACKNOWLEDGEMENTS

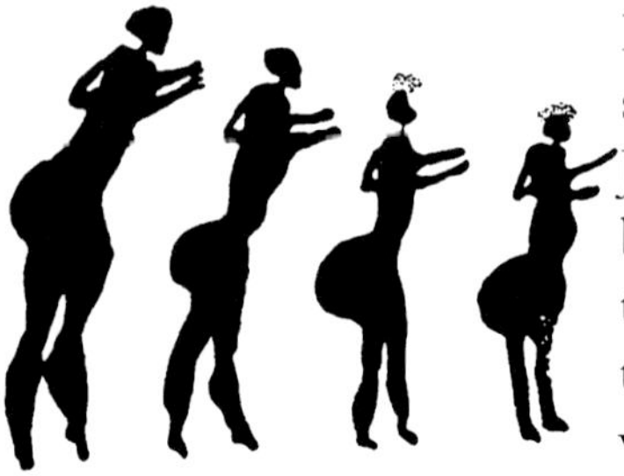

Recording of rock paintings in the Cederberg started in the 1950s when 'Ginger' Townley Johnson, Hym Rabinowitz and Percy Sieff began spending their weekends and holidays in these mountains. I was one of many students they took with them from time to time and I would like to thank them for this enriching experience. They generously donated their information to the Archaeological Data Recording Centre at the South African Museum in Cape Town and we were able to make use of it. Other rock art enthusiasts such as Jalmar and Ione Rudner, Godfrey Hoehn and other members of the South African Archaeological Society, students and staff of the Spatial Archaeology Research Unit at the Department of Archaeology at the University of Cape Town including Royden Yates, Tony Manhire and John Parkington, and Bill van Rijssen, Graham Avery and Mike Wilson at the South African Museum, were equally generous in giving information. David Lewis-Williams and Thomas Dowson from the Rock Art Research Unit at the University of the Witwatersrand have been inspirational and I am very grateful to them too. A general book like this one could not have been written without reference to the published works of all those mentioned above. Their help and encouragement has been greatly appreciated.

When I applied for funding from the Department of Environment Affairs to do a survey of the rock paintings in Forestry Reserves and Wilderness Areas in the Western Cape I was not fully aware of the enormity of the task. I was very fortunate to have been able to employ Stephen Townley Bassett to do the field survey and site recording. He, too, had been introduced to rock art by his uncle, Ginger, and Ginger's companions Hym and Percy, and was making full colour copies of rock paintings as a commercial venture. He proved to be the ideal person for the job and I am very grateful to him for his dedication and for the quality of his recordings.

As Stephen began the foot survey it became obvious that one year was going to be far too short a time and the project was extended for a further year. But even with the extra time, we had to cut the geographic extent of the survey drastically and ended up by focusing only on the Cederberg Wilderness Area and the Groot Winterhoek Wilderness Area. In the Cederberg Stephen was fortunate in having the assistance of Jan Zimri, a field ranger in the Cederberg Wilderness Area, who accompanied him on most of his trips into the mountains and who was responsible for finding many of the sites. We thank him most sincerely for his help.

Thanks are also due to: the numerous other staff members of Cape Nature Conservation and Museums, particularly Afrika de Bruin, Charl du Plessis, Beulah du Plessis, Petrus Hanekom, Adriaan Oosthuizen, Guy Palmer, Gerhard Potgieter, Jaco Rheeder, Kevin Shaw, S W and Marietjie van der Merwe, Jaco van Deventer and Nigel Wessels; the Department of Environment Affairs, and in particular Ingrid Coetzee, Alida van der Merwe and Jacky de Klerk, who were always efficient and helpful; staff and students of the Department of Archaeology at the University of Stellenbosch for providing logistical and moral support in the form of an office, secretarial assistance and help in the field; the University of Stellenbosch Research Grants Division for managing the grant funds; staff of the Geography Department at the University of Stellenbosch for the management of the geographic information system generated for the Cederberg Wilderness Area; and staff and students of the Computer Science Department at the University of Stellenbosch for their much-needed assistance with analysis of the project results.

Since this book was first printed in 1994 my colleagues at the National Monuments Council, in particular Peter Farmer and Ron Martin, have given enthusiastic support to our programme to remove graffiti from rock paintings. I am immensely grateful to them and to other members of the NMC's A-Team for their dedication.

INTRODUCTION

One of the most enduring charms of the Cederberg is the feeling that every time you visit these mountains you will experience something new. The original inhabitants, whose ancestors lived here for tens of thousands of years, saw changes on a daily and seasonal scale. There were also major environmental and cultural adjustments wrought by climatic and social change that took thousands of years to complete. A Greek philosopher, Heraclitus, remarked over 2 500 years ago that one could never step into the same river twice. He meant that the water and the bed in which it flows is ever-changing.

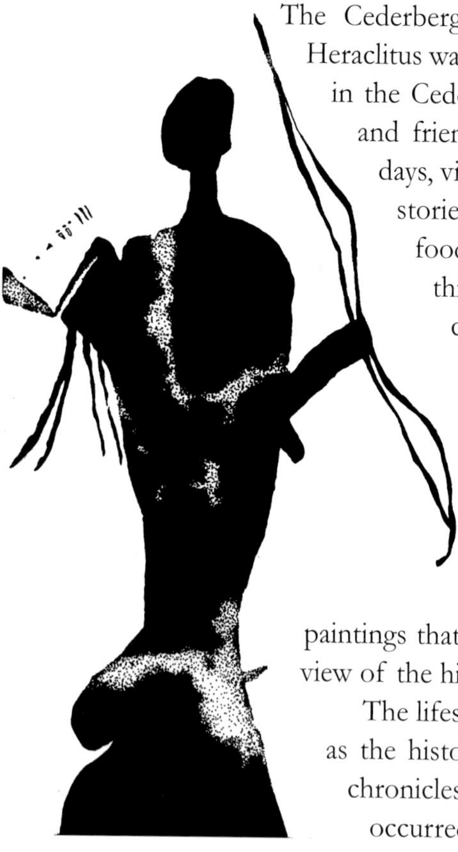

The Cederberg is ever-changing too. At the time that Heraclitus was writing in Greece, the San (Bushmen) lived in the Cederberg and enjoyed the company of family and friends, argued with each other, planned their days, visited the coast or interior, played music, told stories, sang and danced, hunted and foraged for food, made mistakes, discovered new ways to do things, took part in ritual ceremonies and coped with good times and with bad. As was happening in Greece, a few of the San became skilled artists. Instead of painting on the walls of buildings and making marble sculptures, however, the San helped perpetuate their religious beliefs by recording their experiences in paintings on the walls of rock shelters. It is these paintings that are the focus of this book. They record a view of the history of the San in the Cederberg.

The lifestyle of the San was by no means static. Just as the history of people in other parts of the world chronicles changes of one kind another, so changes occurred here too. The descendants of the earliest painters were soon to learn of herding from the *Khoekhoen* (Hottentots) who brought sheep and cattle to southern Africa about 2 000 years ago. Still later, both the San and the Khoekhoen were crushed by rapid upheavals that began about three hundred years ago when the Dutch settled at the Cape. Within less than a century the San were no longer able to maintain their social system, many were killed and others were taken as servants by the European farmers, or moved to the towns.

History, a complex mixture of opinions and viewpoints, is dependent not only on what is recorded by whom, but also on what information survives either through chance or artifice. It is an ongoing debate that can be revised constantly as individuals and generations look back at what has gone before and give their own perspectives. The rock art of the Cederberg has been interpreted and re-interpreted many times over the past century and opinions will no doubt continue to be exchanged and argued over in the future. The following chapters take a look at some of these viewpoints that are current in the 1990s.

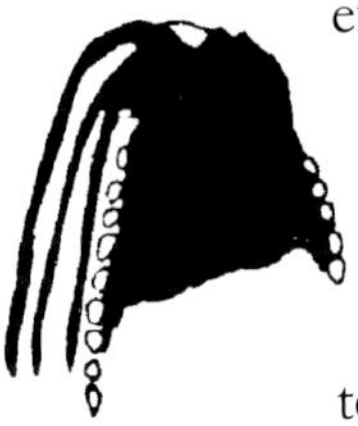

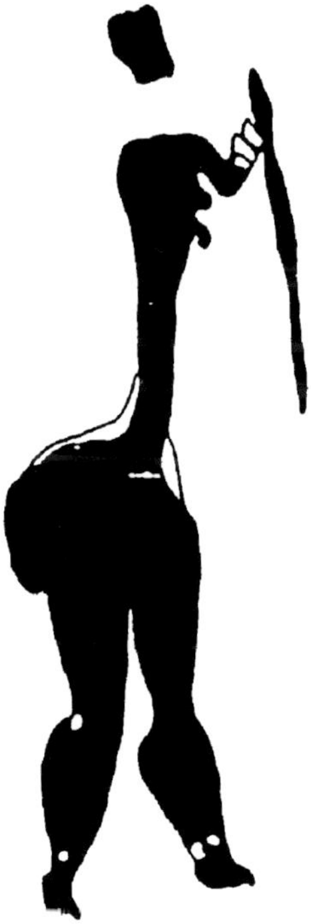

As an example of how the terms of history alter with new viewpoints, take the words 'San' and 'Khoekhoen' which are used to describe the oldest of the indigenous people of South Africa. If this book had been written in the mid-seventeenth century, we would have called the same people 'Sonqua' and 'Quena'. If it had been written fifty years ago, we would have referred to them as 'Bushmen' and 'Hottentots'. But the connotations of these terms are now considered to be uncomplimentary or even offensive. Amongst some communities Bushman and Hottentot are used as insults. Even the current usage of San and Khoekhoen is not unproblematic and may well change again in the years to come.

DEFINITION OF TERMS

Khoisan is a word used to describe both the Khoekhoen and the San, the indigenous Stone Age peoples of South Africa. The Khoisan people themselves did not use this word as they had no need for such a term. It was coined in the 1920s by a German anthropologist who chose the spelling Khoi rather than Khoe and combined it with San. It literally means 'Person-foragers'.

San is an alternative to the term Bushman because of the unflattering connotations the word Bushman has acquired. It is a word from the Nama language (a Khoekhoe group) and is the common gender plural of the word Sa which means a person who forages for food, in other words a hunter-gatherer. By adding the suffix -n it becomes 'forager people'. Unfortunately, the word has acquired the connotation of 'vagabond', rather like the word 'Gypsy' carries unflattering meanings. There has been much debate about the relative merits of the terms 'San' and 'Bushman'. San is currently favoured as a general term to replace Bushman in South Africa, although some of the people who until recently were living as hunter-gatherers in Botswana and Namibia still prefer to call themselves Bushmen. San is preferred in this book.

The San were indigenous southern African people who lived by hunting, fishing and foraging or gathering. Human skeletal remains found at archaeological sites in the southern Cape suggest that people of similar physical type to the San were living in this part of the continent as long as 120 000 years ago.

The hunter-gatherer people whom Van Riebeeck and his colleagues met in the mountains of the south-western Cape in the late seventeenth century referred to themselves as *Sonqua* or *Soaqua*. Like the */Xam* who lived in the Northern Cape, they were a sub-group of the San. The term was used also for people in the southern and eastern Cape. San can be equated in scale with the term 'European' which describes a large number of culturally distinct peoples in western Europe who spoke different languages.

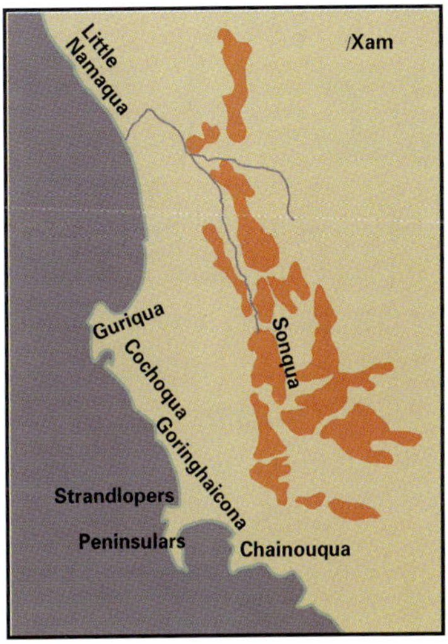

Figure 1
Map showing Khoisan groups in the Western Cape in 1652.

Khoekhoen is the common gender plural for the Nama word 'man' or 'person'. Roughly translated it means 'people' and is also sometimes translated as 'men of men'. It is used to describe all the herder or pastoralist people who were living in southern Africa at the time of European contact. The spelling more accurately pronounces the Nama word and is used here in preference to *Khoikhoin*. The same word in the language of the herders at the Cape in the seventeenth century was spelled by Jan van Riebeeck in his diary as 'Quena'. It is basically the same word whether you pronounce or write it as 'khoi', 'khoe' or 'que'. The difference is that the Nama language doubled the stem and added an 'n' to make the common gender plural, whereas the south-western Cape language group used it singly and added 'na' on the end. Many people today drop the 'n' at the end of Khoekhoen. It should be there if the word is used as a noun, but can be omitted if it is used as an adjective.

The Khoekhoen in the Western Cape included the Goringhaicona, Cochoqua, Guriqua and the Nama or Namaqua (*Figure 1*). They had the same relationship to Khoekhoen as Sonqua and /Xam had to San, and as Swedish and Norwegian have to Scandinavian. San and Khoekhoen had a similar relationship to each other as the Ancient Britons had to the Romans.

The *Later Stone Age* is the last stage of the Stone Age. The Earlier Stone Age dates from more than 1,5 million years until about 200 000 years ago, the Middle Stone Age dates from about 200 000 to about 25 000 years ago and the Later Stone Age dates from 25 000 years to a few hundred years ago. It was during the Later Stone Age that people began making artefacts similar to those used by the Khoisan in recent times.

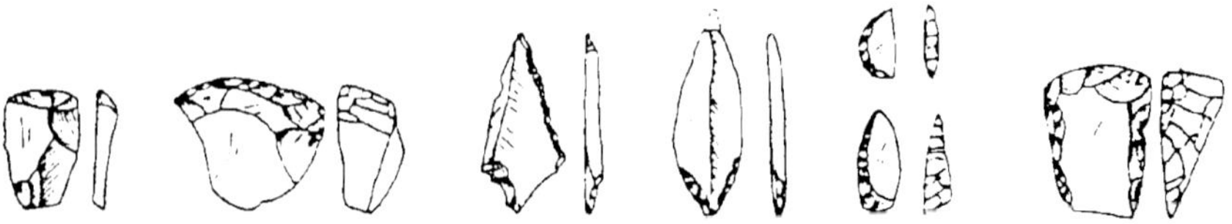

The history of the San in the Western Cape is recorded in part by the rock paintings, but also by the stone artefacts, food remains and other items left at places where they lived. South Africa's Stone Age people, who included the San and their ancestors, made stone tools for well over a million years. Although we can get some idea of their technical ability from these tools, we can tell more about their beliefs from their rock paintings and engravings that were done within the last 20 – 30 000 years. It is only recently that we have begun to unravel the code of these paintings and to discover why they were done and what they mean.

Once we understand the depth of meaning of the rock paintings, and recognise the conventions used by the artists, we realise that the San were no ordinary people. The fact that they did not record their history in the same way as the Greeks did does not mean that they had no history. The contempt and fear expressed by the European visitors and settlers in their own descriptions of the San and Khoekhoen they met at the Cape was born of ignorance. It is easy for us, looking back, to see that had the Europeans been able to befriend the San they would have learned much to their advantage about sharing resources, about herbal medicines and about veld management. It was not so easy for the Trekboers, however, to come to terms with the fact that they were taking the land of the San and that the San had to fight back in any way they could.

But the gun was mightier than the bow and arrow. The Europeans sought to protect their private property and to take possession of the land. Having come from Europe, they considered the land to be unoccupied because the Khoekhoen and the San did not organise themselves and their living space in the same way as Europeans did. They saw the San as robbers and thieves, heathens no better than baboons who deserved to die for their 'crimes'.

The San, on the other hand, wanted to retain a share of their land and believed they should share too in the food and technology that the Europeans brought with them. When the Europeans resisted sharing because they saw it as stealing and antithetical to one of the ten commandments of Christianity, the San retaliated. A /Xam man in the north-western Cape, when asked by a British commissioner in the 1860s why he and his people continued to steal from the colonists, replied poignantly "It is a fight with death either way", for if they did not take the food, they could not eat, and if they could not eat, they would die. This situation was repeated in many regions of southern Africa over the past three centuries and the Cederberg is one of them.

The history of people in the Cederberg can be seen through several windows on the past. One of these windows looks through to the landscape of mountains, streams, flora and fauna, as well as at rock shelters lived in by Stone Age hunter-gatherers. A window that gives a different view is the written record of the early European travellers and settlers who evaluated what they saw in terms of their seventeenth and eighteenth European perspective. Yet another view is that of the people who lived in the Cederberg for thousands of years: the artists who created the rock paintings and left behind evidence of their rich cultural heritage. A fourth window gives a view of the paintings themselves with some pointers on how to interpret them. The last viewpoint is the one of conservation. This is a window that faces the future and that needs to be carefully designed if we are to preserve rock art for future generations to enjoy.

Looking through these imaginary windows we can glimpse views of some of the events and processes that shaped the lives of the people who lived here. They emphasise that people are an integral part of the landscape in which they live and that wilderness areas such as the Cederberg have been walked and used for far longer than we would ordinarily imagine. This book will open each of these windows. It pieces together a view of the past that will help you to understand how rich the San culture was and how we know what we do about it.

A VIEW OF THE LAND

The sedimentary rocks of the Cederberg are part of the Table Mountain Group. This Group is the basal unit of the Cape Supergroup, formed beneath the sea about 500 hundred million years ago. The rocks were subsequently folded some 250 million years ago and uplifted and eroded to form the L-shaped Cape Fold Belt of mountains from Vanrhynsdorp in the north to Cape Town in the south and Grahamstown in the east (*Figure 2*).

The Cederberg is one of many ranges within the Cape Fold Belt. It stretches from just north of the Pakhuis Pass to south of Citrusdal, and from Clanwilliam, Citrusdal and the Olifants River valley in the west to Wuppertal, the Doorn River and the Koue Bokkeveld in the east. The range covers an area of about 130 000 ha, of which 75 000 are incorporated into the Cederberg Wilderness Area and adjacent forestry reserves that are managed by Western Cape Nature Conservation. The range is composed of a series of ridges that run roughly north-south, and valleys that cut into them both from south to north and from east to west. The highest ridge includes the Sneeuberg which rises to 2028 m. Water is an important component of the Cederberg and its abundance led to declaration of the area as a Water Catchment Area in the 1930s.

Geologically, the Table Mountain Group of the Cederberg is composed of five distinct formations: the Peninsula at the base, overlain by the glacial beds of the Pakhuis Formation and then by the shale band of the Cedarberg Formation and finally the Nardouw Subgroup. At least two major advances of the ancient Gondwana ice sheet can be traced in the Pakhuis Formation. The Cedarberg Formation was deposited when the sea level rose again after this glacial period. However, it is the harder quartzite rocks of the underlying Peninsula Formation that have weathered into the most convenient rock shelters and that have preserved rock paintings best. Large standing rocks in the Nardouw Subgroup have also provided sheltered places for people to stay. Rock paintings occur in all the formations.

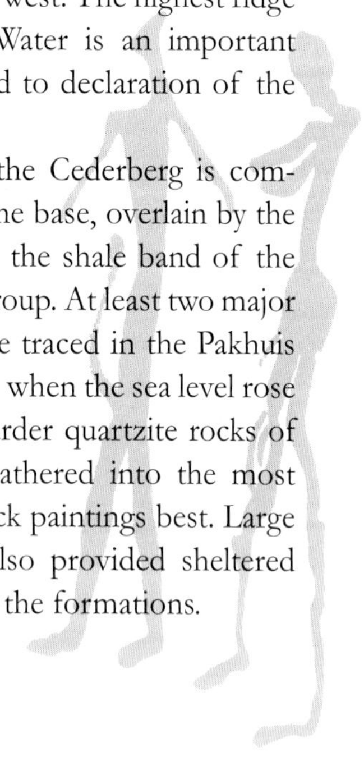

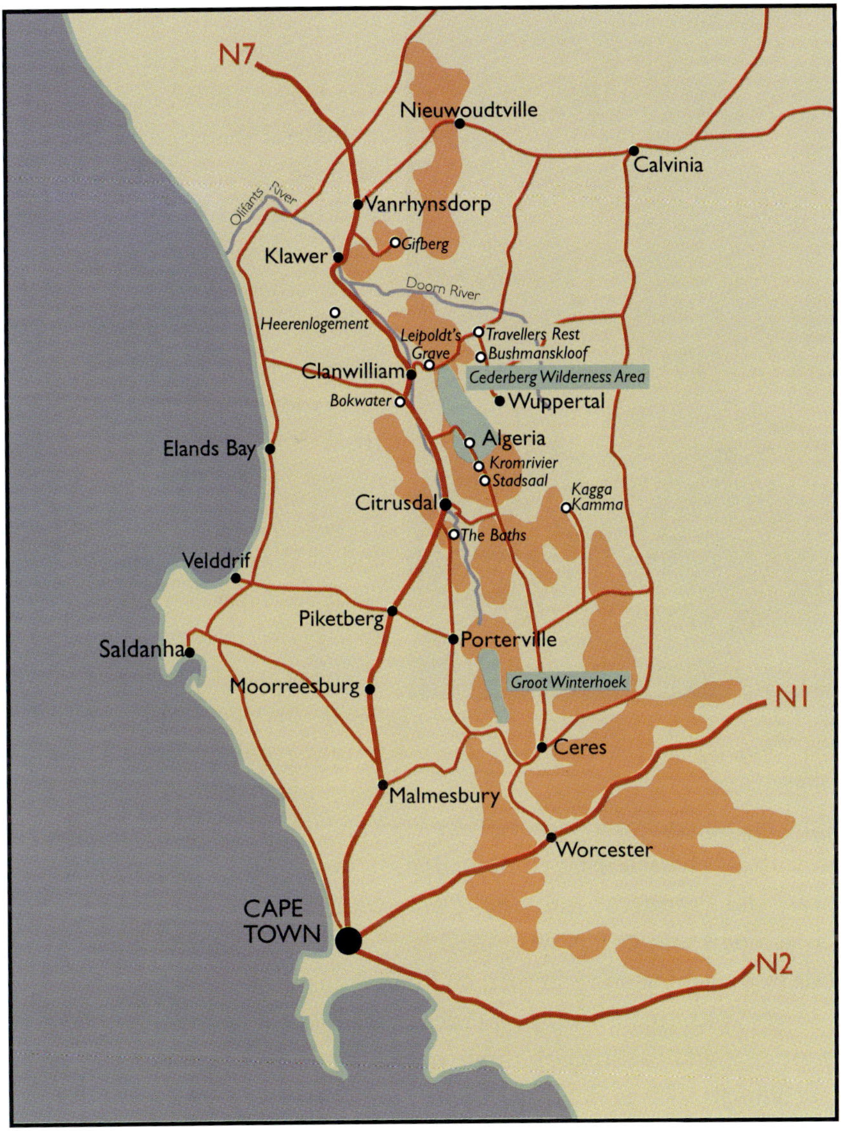

Figure 2
Map of the Western Cape showing the position of the Cederberg mountain chain and other places mentioned in the text. Rock painting sites open to the public are written in italics.

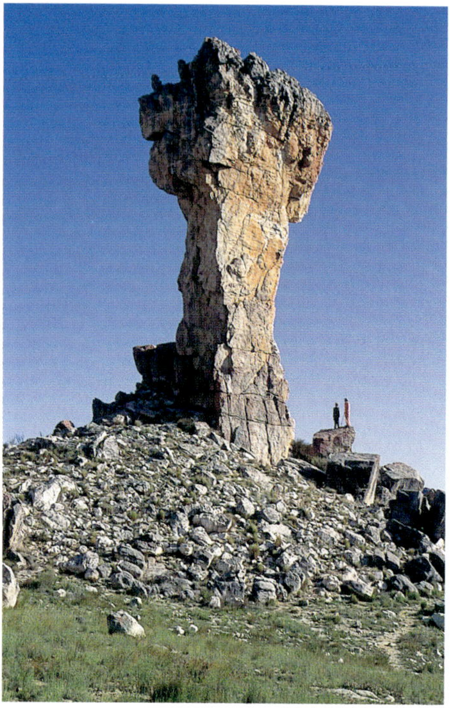

Figure 3
Rock formations in the Cederberg: the Maltese Cross.

Some of the most evocative features of the Cederberg are the weathered rocks in weird and wonderful shapes, now called the Maltese cross (*Figure 3*), the Wolfberg Arch, the Stadsaal, Faith, Hope and Charity, and many others. We can be sure that the San had names for these shapes too. Names such as Krakadouw and Bidouw come from Khoisan words. "Kraka" means "dividing", "douw" means a "pass through the mountains" and "bidouw" or "biedou" is the "milkbush pass" named after a species of *Euphorbia*.

The soils derived from the rocks of the Table Mountain Group, combined with a mediterranean-type climate of hot, dry summers and cool, wet winters, have encouraged mountain fynbos vegetation with its characteristic combination of Restionaceae (reeds), Ericaceae (ericas) and Proteaceae (proteas). Plants with underground storage organs such as bulbs and corms were used by the San and Khoekhoen as staple foods in the spring and summer, and numerous bushes gave edible berries or leaves with medicinal properties. Small antelope such as grysbok, klipspringer and vaal rhebok thrive on mountain fynbos and in the valleys larger animals such as elephant, hippo, eland and others were common until they were shot out by the European hunters. All these animals can be seen in the rock art and were clearly important to the San and Khoekhoen not only as a source of food, but also in their mythology and beliefs.

The range of animals that the painters chose to depict in the rock art bears no relation to the range of animals they ate. Apart from paintings of people, by far the most commonly painted animal in the Cederberg is the eland, followed by the elephant, then by smaller antelope, baboon, zebra, lion and other carnivores. Yet analysis of the bones of animals eaten by Later Stone Age people living in the painted rock shelters shows that their diet was dominated by small antelope such as grysbok and klipspringer and by ground game such as dassie, tortoise and hare. We know, therefore, that here as elsewhere in southern Africa, the rock art does not mirror the fauna of the region. In fact, the rock paintings of the Cederberg include species such as springbok and wildebeest that were not recorded here by European explorers and travellers.

If we are discussing the Cederberg, we cannot escape a note on the cedar trees (*Widdringtonia cedarbergensis*) that can still be seen in some kloofs, but were more common two hundred and more years ago. The official spelling of the Cederberg is after the Dutch who remarked on the magnificent indigenous cedar trees that abounded here. The wood was much sought after by Europeans, but controls had to be instituted from the early 1870s when it became apparent that woodcutters were endangering the species by burning the surrounding vegetation to gain access to the cedars. One astonishing report says that when the telephone line was erected from Piketberg to Clanwilliam, the Cederberg woodcutters provided hundreds and possibly thousands of cedar telephone poles. The long-lasting qualities of cedar wood were certainly known to the San as well.

Apart from providing rocks and rock shelters suitable for paintings, the geology of the Cederberg has another important bearing on the rock art. Bands of iron-rich clays within the Table Mountain Group were hardened over millions of years into rock known as ochre or haematite. This is what the San artists later used for the maroon, red, yellow and orange rock paintings. It was ground into a fine powder and mixed with water, blood or plant juices to make paint. The tiny particles of ochre bond well with the rock and their colour is exceptionally long-lasting.

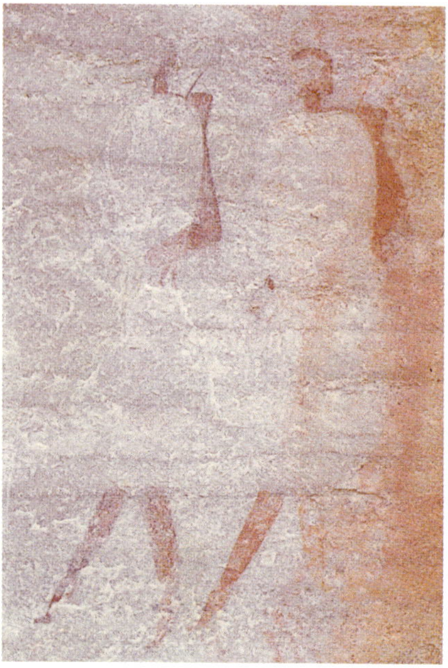

Figure 4
Rock painting of two human figures in which only the red paint remains. The lighter white or yellow paint used for the faces and karosses has faded away.

Black paints were made from manganese oxide or charcoal in the same manner and white paint was made from clay. Neither the black nor the white and yellow bonds as well with the rock as the red paint does and we often find that parts of an animal painted in red have remained while those done in black or white or yellow have left no trace. This happens in particular where people have been painted with white or yellow faces and all that now remains is the top and back of the head which forms a characteristic 'hook head'. The example in *Figure 4* shows the loss not only of the white faces of the two human figures, but the light-coloured karosses or cloaks as well.

The physical properties of the paint have implications for dating the paintings. Radiocarbon dating, the only reliable method available at present, is based on the fact that all living matter, both plant and animal, includes a radiocactive carbon isotope, carbon-14, in equilibrium with the atmosphere. When the plant or animal dies, this radioactive isotope begins to decay at a fixed and known rate. Dating laboratories therefore measure the amount of carbon-14 left in a sample and then calculate how long it has been dead by comparing the level of carbon-14 remaining with that in the atmosphere. Dates are expressed as years BP, i.e. Before the Present. The 'Present' is taken for convenience as AD 1950. Because most of the paintings in South Africa were made with ochre (*Figure 5*), which is not derived from living matter, they cannot be dated. However, paint with charcoal as an ingredient can be dated and a sample from a black painting in the Cederberg has given a date of 500 BP or AD 1450. Such analyses are not done often because they can destroy the painting and because black paint still thick enough to include enough charcoal for dating is uncommon.

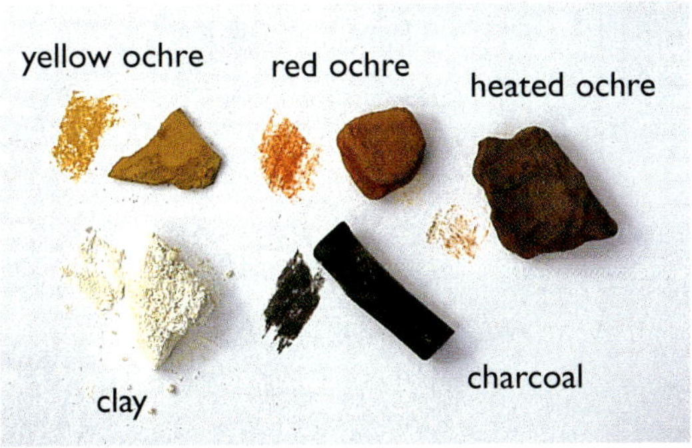

Figure 5
Samples of pigments and the colours they make.

Another way of dating rock art can be used if the painting or engraving was done on a loose stone that was left on the surface of a rock shelter and was subsequently covered by later layers of soil. Charcoal, bone or shell associated with the painted or engraved stone can then be radiocarbon dated. This method was used to date several small rock slabs with paintings found about 0,5 m below the surface in a rock shelter in southern Namibia. The charcoal associated with these paintings was about 27 500 years old. Other painted stones found at four different rock shelters in the southern Cape and associated with artefacts of the Later Stone Age have been dated by the same method to between about 6 200 and 2 000 BP. These dates suggest that the rock art tradition in the Cape is thousands rather than hundreds of years old.

Most researchers believe that the paintings still visible on the rocks of the Cederberg and the western Cape were done within the last six or seven thousand years. This estimate is based both on the dates for painted stones in the southern Cape and on archaeological excavations in rock shelters in the Cederberg. These show that, with one exception, all the Later Stone Age occupations date within the last 7 000 years. There is a period between the last Middle Stone Age occupation more than 30 000 years ago and the first Later Stone Age traces at about 7 000 years ago for which we have no evidence of human occupation in the Cederberg and adjacent river valleys.

Most of this time of apparent non-occupation coincides with cold and dry conditions of the last glacial period. Between 10 000 and about 7 000 years ago there was a time of ecological adjustment to gradual global warming up to temperatures approximately similar to those of the present. The implication is that the Cederberg was not a favoured place to stay when annual temperatures were between 3 and 5 degrees C cooler than at present.

At the other end of the time scale, the most recent rock paintings in the western Cape can be dated by their subject matter because they include horses, ox-wagons, people with guns and even a sailing ship – all indicative of contact with Europeans within the last 350 years.

Apart from these very practical aspects of providing suitable surfaces, raw materials and methods of dating, the physical landscape of the Cederberg has had a powerful symbolic meaning to the people who have lived there. We know from ethnographic records that the San had a strong attachment to the land. They had myths and legends about landscape features such as mountain tops, rock formations and water sources. Nineteenth century /Xam San from the north-western Cape had expressions such as "My heart stands in the hill" and "I am a Brinkkop [hilltop] man" which emphasise their empathy with the landscape. Particular places were used for ceremonies and rituals and many of the place names in South Africa are direct translations of Khoisan names that refer to this practice. The ubiquitous name Elandsfontein may well refer to the numerous springs where rain animals, often eland, were caught. The association between legends and landscape features is very likely to have had an effect on rock art too. The high incidence of eland and elephant in the rock paintings of the Cederberg records not only the fact that they occurred here, but also the symbolic role they played in San beliefs.

The effect of the landscape can still be seen today. In a questionnaire answered by nearly 350 visitors to the Cederberg Wilderness Area in 1992, more than 80% cited the scenery as their major reason for coming there.

A VIEW FROM THE WRITTEN RECORD

The written records of European experiences from the late fifteenth to the late eighteenth century in the south-western Cape describe three main groups of people who were living here when the travellers and settlers from the northern hemisphere arrived by sea. Collectively the local people can be referred to as the Khoisan, but distinctions were made amongst them. They share similar 'click' languages and are genetically more like each other than any other group, but a division is and was made on the basis of economy. *Figure 1* summarises historical information on the geographic distribution of various Khoekhoen and San groups in the Western Cape at the time of European contact.

- The **Khoekhoen** kept both sheep and cattle but also hunted, fished and collected plant foods. Groups amongst them spoke slightly different dialects and were under the leadership of people whom the Europeans called Captains or Chiefs. The Khoekhoen occupied the coastal plain between the Cape Fold Belt mountains and the sea from the Orange River in the north-west to what is today the Eastern Cape in the south-east. Linguists believe that the language of the Khoekhoen in the Cape belongs to the same family as that spoken by Tshu-Khwe in Botswana who, until recently, lived by hunting and gathering. It is therefore hypothesised that the Tshu-Khwe-speaking ancestors of the Cape Khoekhoen acquired domestic stock from neighbouring Iron Age people in south-eastern Africa a little over 2000 years ago. For reasons we do not know, they moved gradually southwards across the Orange River. Archaeological research shows that they were already settled along the west coast in the Northern Cape 2000 years ago.

- The people who Van Riebeeck called '**Strandlopers**' or 'Watermen' were formerly Khoekhoen but became entrepreneurs in the trade between the Dutch and other Khoekhoen. They appear to have been a relatively recent social group that was confined to the vicinity of the Cape Peninsula. As facilitators of trade between visiting ships and Khoekhoen herders, they frequently had no sheep and cattle of their own but they learned European languages well enough to barter with the sailors and continued to fish and collect shellfish. The word 'Strandloper' should therefore not be used as a general term for people who lived along the entire South African coast.

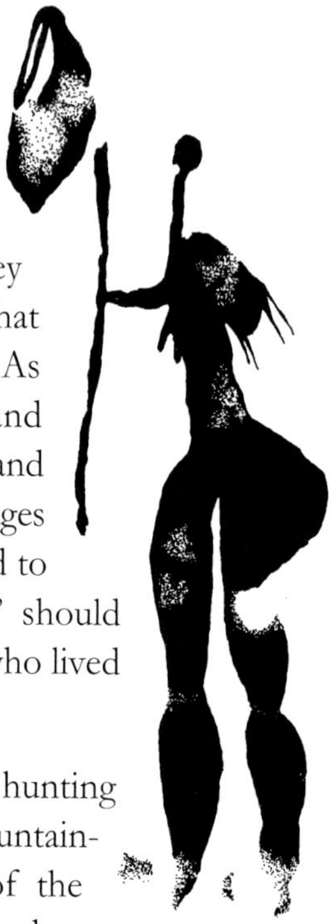

- The **San** did not have sheep or cattle and lived by hunting and gathering, or foraging, mostly in the more mountainous areas. Their language was distinct from that of the Khoekhoen and there is good evidence to suggest that they were the original inhabitants of the region and that they had exploited food resources along the coast in the past. Apart from not owning domesticated animals and speaking a different language, the San were also distinguished by their physical appearance. A difference frequently remarked on by the Dutch was that the San were much shorter than the Khoekhoen. This was probably related to diet as the Khoekhoe children had the benefit of regular supplies of milk and could therefore grow taller on average than their San counterparts.

These groupings of people had some relevance for the Dutch who were trading with the Khoekhoen, but a close reading of the written records suggests that the economic divisions were less clear than the descriptions imply. As San rather than Khoekhoe beliefs are connected with rock art, the implications of these social divisions are relevant if we are to understand who did the rock paintings in the region.

It seems likely that when the herders came to the Cape, they began recruiting resident hunter-gatherers as herdsmen, and indeed the historical records show that San were employed by the Khoekhoen to look after stock. As a result, the Dutch often had difficulty in assigning individual Khoisan to one group or another and more than once referred to 'Bosjesman-Hottentots', or identified people they met according to whether or not they had cattle or sheep. For this reason, some researchers such as Carmel Schrire and Shula Marks would prefer to draw no dividing line between the 'pure' hunter-gatherers at one end of the scale and the 'pure' herders at the other, simply because of the wide range of combinations that were described in the written records.

Others believe that the social structure of hunter-gatherers and herders is so different that they could not have merged. Inheritance, for example, plays an important part in Khoekhoe society where stock is passed on to the next generation on the death of the owner. In San society, on the other hand, there is no inheritance as wealth is not accumulated. Whatever their social and economic differences and similarities, by the late seventeenth century some of the San in the mountains of the western and south-western Cape still retained a separate identity from the Khoekhoen after more than 1 000 years of contact. By contrast, other individuals and families were moving from herding to hunting and gathering, and back again, with apparent ease, and yet others were totally acculturated. This suggests that the process of change from hunting and gathering to herding was on-going, but was by no means complete. Hunter-gatherers in the Cederberg retained their belief system and it remained different from that of the herders at least until the mid-eighteenth century.

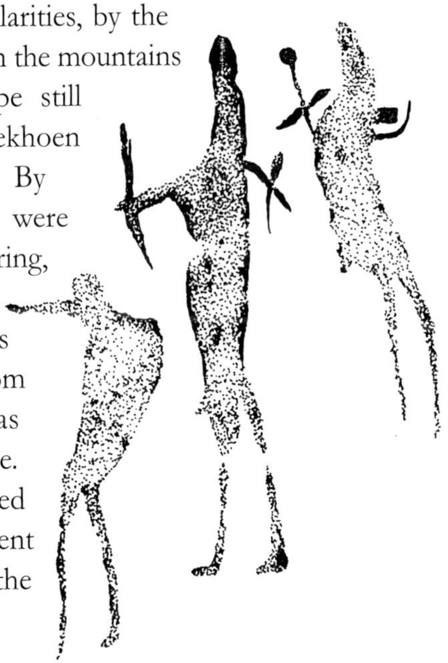

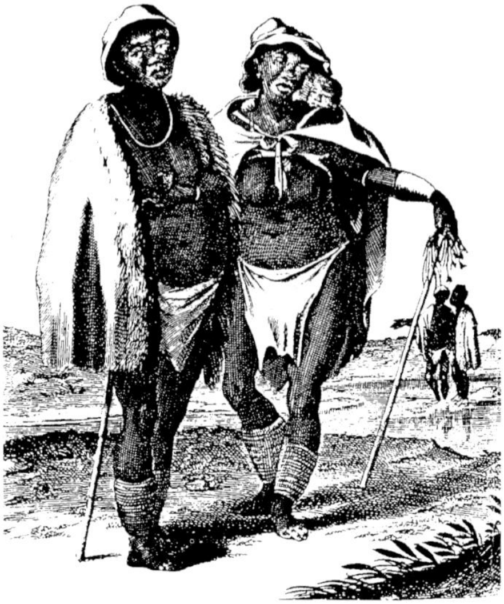

Figure 6
Khoekoen of the Western Cape depicted by an artist for O. Dapper (1668)

After the initial discovery of the sea route around the southern tip of Africa by Bartholomeu Dias in 1487 to 1488, one of the main reasons for Europeans stopping off at the Cape was the presence of the Khoekhoen who had both sheep and cattle to barter. The meat was vital to the health of the sailors and the Khoekhoen, initially unaware of the value of their stock, were eager to exchange their animals for trifling quantities of iron nails, copper ornaments and glass beads. Their love of brass arm and leg ornaments is shown in a seventeenth century drawing of Khoekhoen at the Cape (*Figure 6*). Tobacco and spirits were also popular trade items.

But trade with the Khoekhoen did not necessarily lead to friendship. The Europeans, convinced of their own superiority, were scornful of the Khoekhoe lifestyle and ignorant of their religion. Wouter Schouten who visited the Cape in 1665 wrote:

> But more wonderful was to see the wild nature of the people of the Cabo de Bon Esperance, who because of their beastliness bear no resemblance to mankind … They know nothing of the preparing of food, of agriculture or fishing, of houses or vehicles, and ate no grain … I could notice little or no signs of religion among them…

He was misinformed on almost all counts for the people he described were in fact skilled herdsmen who trained their cattle and knew every one by name. They were expert fishermen, had well designed mat-covered houses, rode on oxen and had a religion that served them extremely well. Schouten went on to describe a dance that almost certainly had a religious purpose:

> sometimes a whole assembly of men, women and children, each clad in a stinking beast-skin, appear in a large pit, cave or other terrifying place, where these wild people make many strange antics, with singing, leaping and dancing, as also with continual hand-clapping. Meanwhile they sometimes turn their eyes to heaven, and then with a red stone write stripes and crosses on each others' foreheads after which each of this lovely brotherhood goes his way.

Schouten was not alone in his lack of understanding of Khoisan lifestyle and beliefs. His views are typical of those of his contemporaries and emphasise for us from the perspective of the twentieth century just how much information about the Khoekhoen was lost and went unrecorded in the written record. This excerpt gives tantalising information about the use of ochre as body paint, but does not mention its use by the Khoekhoen for rock painting. If only we could travel back in a time machine and ask a few questions!

A few of the Khoekhoen learned English and Dutch and realised that the Europeans were purchasing the sheep and cattle below their market value, but were powerless to turn the tide. Within fifty years after the Dutch East India Company established their refreshment station at the Cape in 1652, Khoekhoen society was under considerable pressure. Starrenberg, travelling between the Berg River and Klawer in 1705 commented:

> I have realised with regret how the whole country has been spoilt by the recent freedom of bartering [i.e. with the Dutch colonists], and the atrocities committed by the vagabonds ... and so from men who sustained themselves quietly by cattle-breeding, living in peace and contentment divided under their chiefs and kraals, they have nearly all become Bushmen, hunters and brigands, dispersed everywhere between and in the mountains.

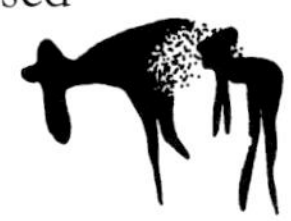

Starrenberg's use of the word Bushman as a synonym for brigands was another sign of the times. The presence of the San was not apparently known to the Dutch until several years after 1652. After their first meeting, Jan van Riebeeck described a group met by Jan Wintervogel in 1655 in the vicinity of present-day Malmesbury:

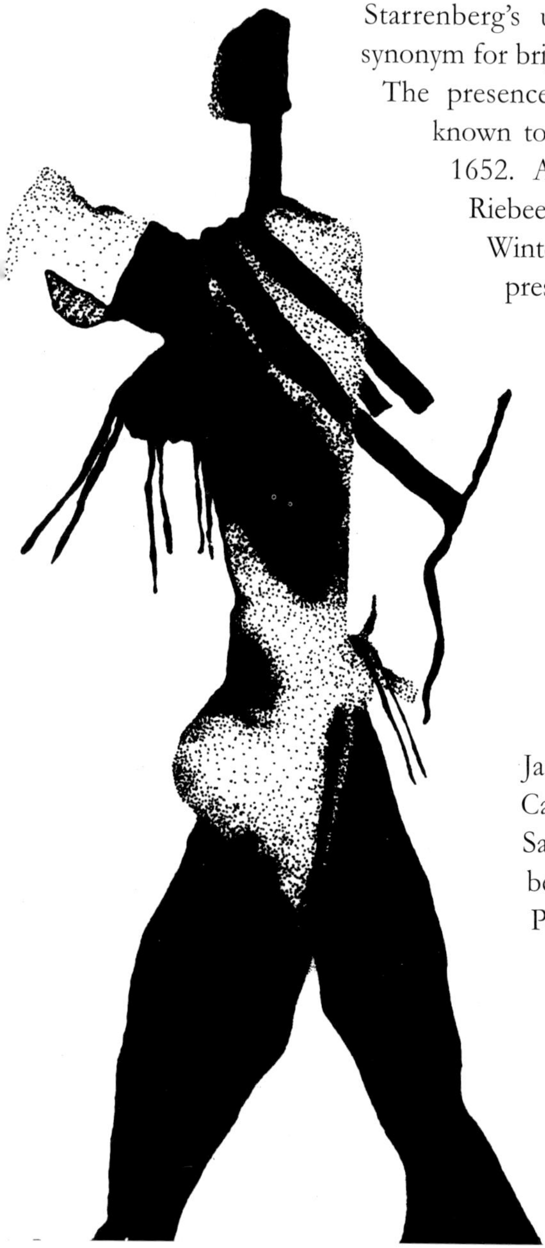

> These men reported that they had been inland about 50 miles to the north from here, where they had come across a certain people of very small stature, subsisting very meagrely, quite wild, without huts, cattle or anything in the world, clad in small skins like these Hottentots and speaking almost as they do.

Jan Danckaert, exploring north of Cape Town in December 1660, met San again, this time at Sonquasdrift between present-day Wellington and Porterville:

> They had come across a poverty-stricken band of tiny people, who had helped them to cross the first range and had been very friendly to them, giving them some honey and dried fish. These small

> people, who have already been encountered somewhat nearer here by previous exploring parties, live in a state of poverty in shabby, low huts made of branches. Our explorers had found some of these standing empty here and there and it seemed to them that these little fellows use them during the night. They are well provided with bows and arrows, and they are adept at using these for shooting all kinds of game for food. Honey also forms part of their diet. They dress like the Hottentots, but they use very poor skins of wild animals.

A short distance further, three more Soaqua ran away from them in fear and left their belongings which included a skin, a bag with roasted dassies and one with honey. A few years later, Simon van der Stel met several groups of people without sheep or cattle in the Berg River valley in 1685 and he also referred to them as Soaqua or Sonqua. They were armed with poisoned arrows and spears.

Unlike the Khoekhoen, though, the San were not singled out for portraits by European travellers, and indeed there is remarkably little information about them in the seventeenth century records. We have usually explained this by saying that the San were very shy of contact with Europeans. It may also have been that they preferred to live in more mountainous areas where the Europeans did not explore.

The mention by Van Riebeeck of two groups of people at the Cape in the seventeenth century, the hunter-gatherer Sonqua and the pastoralist Khoekhoen, has emphasised the differences he perceived. But there were also many similarities in the lifestyle of the Khoisan people at this time. The Khoekhoen kept sheep and cattle for milk and meat, but, like the hunter-gatherers, still gathered plant foods from the veld. Both hunted game animals and both ate fish and shellfish on the coast and along the rivers inland. Both used bows and arrows and made stone and bone tools. Although the Khoekhoen had copper and iron artefacts and ornaments too, they did not smelt the metals themselves but traded them from the Bantu-speaking farmers to the east and north-east and, later, from the Europeans.

Several archaeologists and historians believe that individuals amongst the Khoisan moved freely from being hunter-gatherers to herders and that by the time of European colonisation the terms San and Khoekhoen were useful merely to describe opposite ends of a continuum. They are drawn to this conclusion because similarities between San and Khoekhoe lifestyles and artefacts do not make it easy to recognise herders and 'pure' hunter-gatherers in the archaeological record. Despite this, some archaeologists believe it can be done. Professor Andrew Smith, for example, has concluded that hunting people continued to live separately from herders at the Cape until well after European settlement. By denying hunters access to domesticated stock, he argues that the herders kept them on the fringes of pastoralist society in a subservient status.

In the eighteenth century both the Khoekhoen and the San in the south-western Cape eventually fell victim to the European settlers. Danckaert and Van der Stel went on exploratory expeditions through the Berg and Olifants River valleys in the late seventeenth century but European farmers only settled in the Olifants River valley from the 1720s. This was after the power of the Khoekhoen had been undermined by the smallpox epidemic which began in February 1713 and by diseases that decimated their flocks and herds after 1714. The 'Bushman War' of 1739 was a series of engagements in which Khoekhoe resistance was effectively crushed south of Namaqualand and the Olifants River mouth, and west of the Doorn River. This encouraged the Trekboers to move further north and eastwards. In their wake the so-called Bastaard farmers were able to hold on to land in the Cederberg until late in the eighteenth century.

By the early nineteenth century the take-over by Europeans was complete and there is no record of Khoisan living independently as hunter-gatherers or herders in the mountains of the Cederberg after that time. Their descendants were settled on mission stations such as Wuppertal and were employed on European-owned farms and in the towns and villages.

A VIEW OF THE ARTISTS

If the San and Khoekhoe culture and lifestyles had indeed merged, what evidence is there that the San remained the only artists after the Khoekhoen arrived in the Western Cape? And what do we know about the lifestyle of the artists? There are views about this that can be seen in written records, in the results of archaeological excavations and in the paintings.

The written records

The first European traveller to remark in print on the occurrence of rock paintings in South Africa was Ensign Beutler who went to the Eastern Cape in 1752, a full century after Van Riebeeck settled at the Cape. It was also more than 60 years after Simon Van der Stel's expedition went north to Namaqualand and purportedly camped in the rock shelter known as the Heerenlogement (*Figure 7*) where some faded rock paintings are still to be seen today. It is intriguing to speculate on why Van der Stel did not think to mention them.

Once travellers began to record the presence of rock paintings and rock engravings, they were remarkably consistent in assigning authorship to the San rather than to the Khoekhoen. One could argue that most of these accounts are from the Drakensberg where the Khoekhoen did not have a strong presence in the nineteenth century, but even in the northern Cape where the Korana and other Khoekhoen groups lived, it was the San who were said to be the artists.

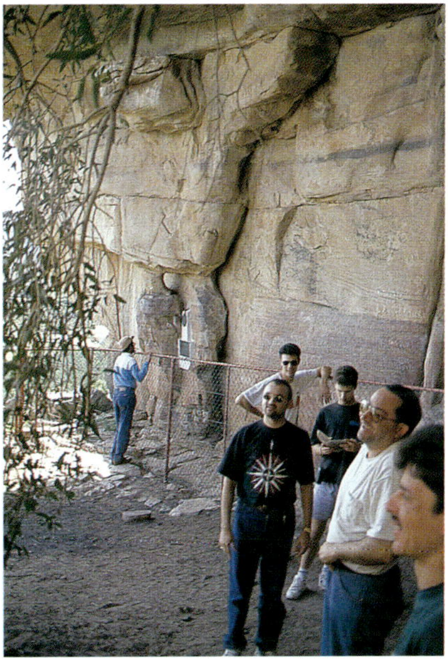

Figure 7
The Heerenlogement today.

Three /Xam San men who had been living in Bushmanland in the Northern Cape in the second half of the nineteenth century provided invaluable testimony about the rock art tradition of their people. The written record of their folklore, beliefs and life stories was compiled by Dr Wilhelm Bleek and his sister-in-law Dr Lucy Lloyd in Cape Town in the 1870s and 1880s. The men had been arrested for stock theft and culpable homicide after the turmoil of the Korana War of 1868/69 when ownership of the land between the Sak and the Orange rivers was contested. The British had annexed the land in 1847 and allowed stock farmers to obtain ownership. The /Xam San and the Korana Khoekhoen challenged this ownership in a series of skirmishes but were finally overcome by the British Northern Border Police who arrested hundreds of people. Those convicted of crimes were sent to the Breakwater Prison in Cape Town. Dr Bleek, anxious to learn something of the San language, obtained permission to interview them. Those who knew most about their language and folklore each spent several years at the Bleek family home in Mowbray.

The /Xam informants knew a little Dutch and with this as a starting point Bleek and Lloyd learned their language, worked out a method for recording the clicks and other sounds that had no equivalent in English, and began writing down verbatim what they were told. They then translated the /Xam into English and built up over 11 000 pages of testimony. Bleek died in 1875, but Lloyd continued interviewing /Xam until 1884 when she and Bleek's widow went to Germany to enable the Bleek daughters to be educated. They returned to South Africa in about 1904 and Lucy Lloyd taught her niece, Dorothea Bleek, to take over the work of translation and publication. Dorothea Bleek later travelled to Kenhardt and Prieska to try to trace the relatives and descendants of the /Xam but found that they no longer knew the language and could remember no stories.

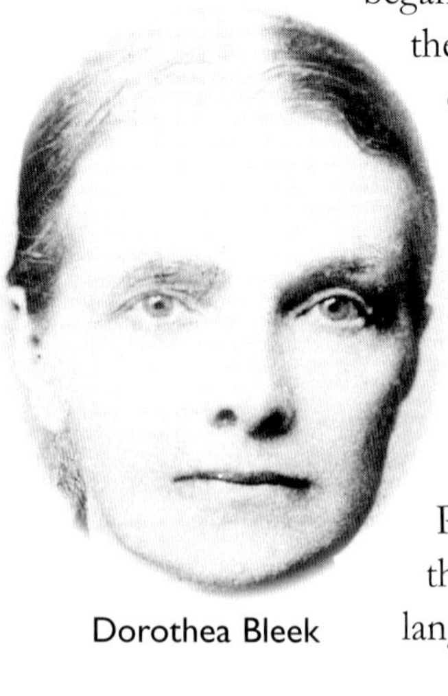
Dorothea Bleek

The Victorian community in Cape Town in the late nineteenth century was very interested in such topics as the Bushmen and their rock art. Indeed, Lucy Lloyd and her contemporaries did their best to encourage farmers to send in records of rock art on their property so that a list could be compiled. Others, such as George Stow, Joseph Orpen and Edward Dunn, also spoke to San they met in the country and recorded what they knew of the rock paintings and engravings. Copies were made of the art and some were published in magazines while others were held in private collections. Some of these copies were shown to the /Xam men living at the Bleek home and their comments make fascinating reading.

Dr Bleek himself was convinced from these interviews that the rock paintings were not merely "daubing of figures for idle pastime, but ... a truly artistic conception of the ideas which most deeply moved the Bushman mind, and filled it with religious feelings." His views were not promoted by others after his untimely death and it was not until further detailed interviews were conducted with San in Botswana and Namibia a century later that the full import of his words was realised.

Patricia Vinnicombe and David Lewis-Williams were the first to get an inkling of the importance of the Bleek and Lloyd records and the way in which they could be combined with the information given by modern San to better understand the meaning of the rock art. Despite the fact that the /Xam had lived in an area where there are no rock paintings, only rock engravings, and that most of the San in Botswana had never done either paintings or engravings because they lived in the Kalahari far away from suitable rocks and rock shelters, their religious beliefs and rituals were essentially similar. They also gave similar explanations for copies of rock paintings they were shown. These similarities are indicative of a belief system with elements that were common to all San in southern Africa in the past. We can therefore use the written records made by Bleek and Lloyd and by twentieth century ethnographers and anthropologists to discover something of the meaning of the images that the San artists chose to portray in their paintings and engravings.

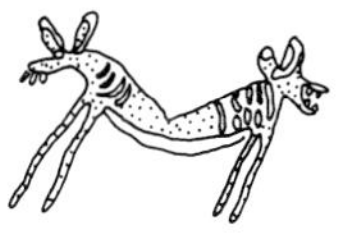

Archaeological information

Archaeologists try to work out what happened in the past by carefully excavating and analysing the non-perishable artefacts and food remains left at sites where people lived. About ten Stone Age living sites have been excavated in the Cederberg and surrounding areas over the past 30 years and there are many more sites in the open and in rock shelters that have been recorded. The accumulated results show that although people began living in the Cederberg during the Earlier Stone Age about 500 000 years ago, they did not live there continuously. There are signs of Middle Stone Age occupation in the mountains as well. They can probably be assigned to the period between about 125 000 and about 40 000 years ago on the basis of the kinds of stone artefacts found.

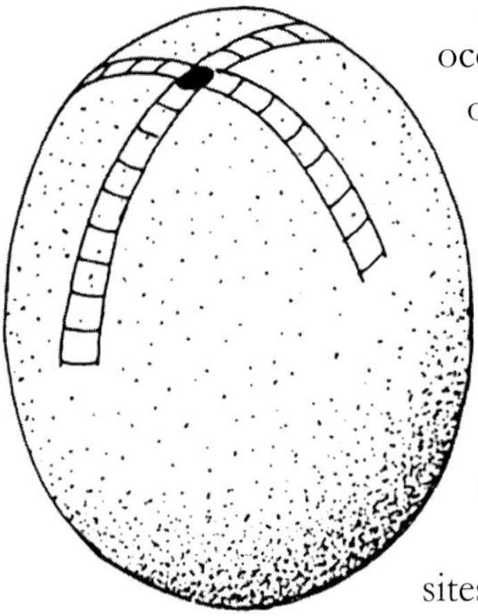

The most common archaeological sites are those occupied by Later Stone Age people, the ancestors of the modern San. In southern Africa the Later Stone Age began about 25 000 years ago. It was at this time that the range of artefacts made by the San at the time of European contact was first introduced. These include ostrich eggshell beads, ostrich eggshell water containers, tortoiseshell bowls, polished bone points and small stone tools.

In the Cederberg area, the Later Stone Age sites excavated so far date from about 8 000 years ago and it is from this time onwards that it is believed that the rock paintings were done. Later Stone Age people at this time were hunting with bows and arrows and traps, they made quivers of bark and leather to store their hunting equipment, they used digging sticks weighted with bored stones, they carried their food and equipment in leather bags, they made clothing from leather, and they decorated themselves with ostrich eggshell and marine shell beads. Their artefacts were made of stone, bone, shell and wood.

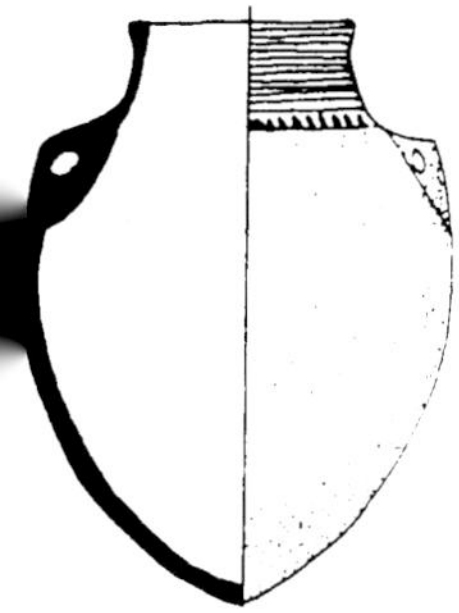

The ancestors of the Khoekhoen, who first came to the Western Cape about 2 000 years ago, also made stone, wood, shell and bone tools. They made and used ostrich eggshell water containers and beads, leather clothing and bags. Like the San, they also gathered plant foods and hunted game. They differed from the San in that they introduced new artefacts in the form of fired clay pots, which were used to store their dairy produce, and metal artefacts which they traded from Iron Age people to the east and north.

Although we know that the Khoekhoen should be recognisable archaeologically by their pottery and the bones of their domesticated animals, identifying individual sites as San or Khoekhoen on the basis of the artefacts and bones of hunted animals has proved difficult. We have only circumstantial evidence to suggest that the two groups made different stone tools. Furthermore, the San undoubtedly traded pottery, sheep and cattle from the Khoekhoen so the presence of these items at a site is no guarantee that the Khoekhoen lived there. One way to distinguish Khoekhoe herder sites from San hunter-gatherer ones is by their settlement pattern. Open sites with large numbers of sheep and cattle bones are likely to have been occupied by Khoekhoen, whereas smaller rock shelter sites in the mountains were more likely to have been occupied by the San.

Some sites are not easily classified, but the weight of evidence we have accumulated indicates that the Khoekhoen were not living in the mountains on a regular basis, but on the coastal plain where the grazing was better. This is not to say that they did not visit the mountains. They may well have done so in small groups on hunting and collecting expeditions. The implications for the question of authorship of the paintings are that there is no clear-cut geographical separation of the San and Khoekhoen that coincides with the distribution of rock art. Paintings occur throughout the mountains and the coastal plain. The rock art tradition was in place both on the coastal plain and in the mountains before the advent of the Khoekhoen and their sheep and cattle, and it persisted after their arrival as well.

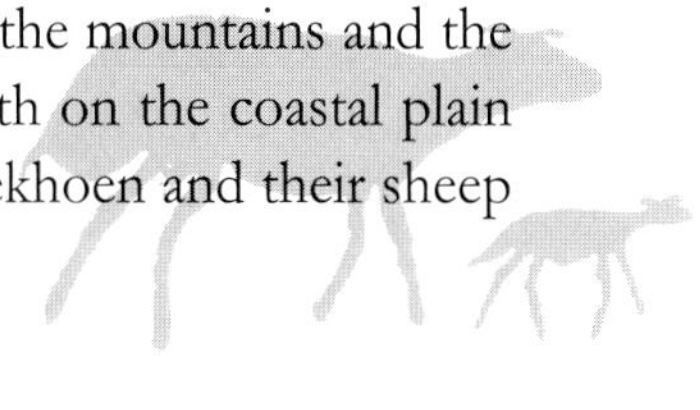

The paintings

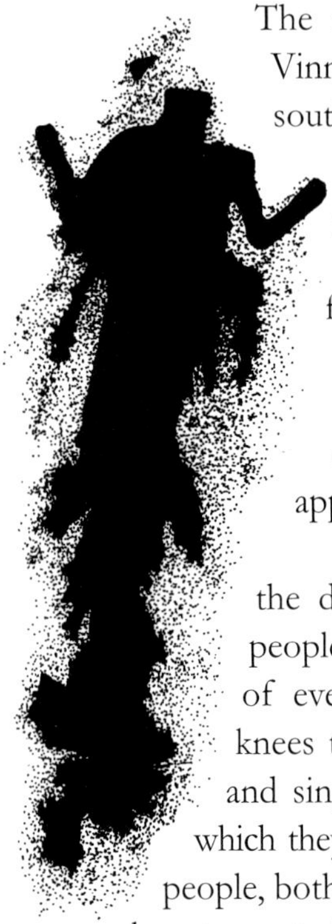

The most important discovery in the research done by Vinnicombe, Lewis-Williams, Dowson and others is that southern African San rock art is essentially religious in nature. The choice of subject matter, the way in which it is painted, where it is placed, details of posture and composition, and the non-reality of many images are all features related to the religious experiences of the artists. Although we will probably never be able to interpret fully all rock paintings and engravings, once we know the context in which they were done we can come closer to appreciating the depth of their meaning.

San religion, like many other religions, is centred around the desire for supernatural power or inspiration to enable people to cope better with the social and economic problems of everyday life. Whereas Christians may get down on their knees to pray silently to God, the San used dancing, clapping and singing to enter into an altered state of consciousness in which they would receive supernatural power. Shamans or medicine people, both men and women, learned how to receive this power and how to control and use it. One San man described the power as similar to electricity: if it is properly controlled and used in small quantities it can be very beneficial, but if it is not controlled it can be deadly.

The San shamans used power received during trance for three main purposes. One was to heal people. The shaman in trance would lay hands on the ailing person and smear them with his or her nasal blood and sweat generated during dancing. The 'arrows of sickness' could then be drawn out and discarded. Another purpose was to make rain. The rainmaker's spirit would leave his or her body and search out an imaginary rain animal from a water hole or from a mountain top. The rain animal would be led, often with a thong, across the veld and where it was killed and the blood or milk spilled, there it would rain. The rain animal could take many forms from an eland, a hippopotamus or an elephant, to an unidentifiable beast. Large, fat, docile rain animals would make soft 'female' rain and fiercer rain animals that resisted capture would make thunderstorms or 'male' rain. A third purpose of trance was to allow the shaman's spirit to go on out-of-body travel to seek out and control game animals or to find and observe absent friends and relatives. When entering such a state, the shaman would sometimes take the form of a malevolent animal such as a lion, or may feel as though he or she was flying, or travelling through water or underground.

The research done by Lewis-Williams and Dowson led them to investigate the experiences of those who enter altered states of consciousness. Published descriptions of trances and visions by many who have taken hallucinogenic drugs suggest that all people, regardless of age, creed and nationality, tend to have remarkably similar experiences. This is because every human brain is 'wired' in the same way, regardless of when and where one was born or educated. There are various intensities of trance that range from an early stage in which one sees patterns of light as dots, grids, spirals, boat-shapes, and so on, to hallucinations of real and imaginary people, animals and objects. In the deepest trance, people describe feeling drawn into the vision and becoming part of it. The patterns of light are superimposed on the visions and it is difficult to distinguish what is real and what is not.

Although there will always be a few dissenting voices that claim a foreign influence on South African rock art, there is no doubt that the majority of the rock paintings in the Cederberg, and in the rest of southern Africa, were done by the San and their ancestors. The connections between the images in the rock paintings and the San beliefs recorded by Bleek and Lloyd in the nineteenth century, and by anthropologists further north in the twentieth century, are convincing evidence for a well-developed and sophisticated religious art tradition.

What could be questioned is the circumstances that led to the painting tradition, and whether there is any reason to suppose that the Khoekhoen may have done some of the paintings too. These questions cannot be answered directly by reference to written records because there is no reliable written record on the subject. None of the early travellers in this region mention the presence of either painters or paintings.

Without ethnographic clues we can make many mistakes. Initially, for example, it was thought that because some paintings of people show them to be tall, they must be Khoekhoen. When paintings of fat-tailed sheep, the kind kept by the Khoekhoen, were seen, it was again assumed that the Khoekhoen had painted them. Both of these conclusions have been shown to be spurious. We know now that elongation was a sensation felt by the painters during trance and is not a literal depiction. We also know that although there are written records confirming that San had been rock artists elsewhere in South Africa, there are no such references for the Khoekhoen.

In the absence of methods to date the paintings directly, clues to the relative age of paintings can be drawn from a careful analysis of which images are consistently found on top of others. Where this occurs, we could argue that those on top were done more recently than those below. Bill van Rijssen, formerly an archaeologist at the South African Museum, noticed that human handprints (*Figure 8*) are consistently found overlying images of people and animals in the south-western Cape. He also noted that smears, finger dots and crude paintings done with a finger rather than a brush – he called them sematographs – are more often associated with handprints than with any other images. He then studied the distribution of handprints and found that out of a sample of 120 rock shelters with handprints in the south-western Cape, about 80 were located at 300 m or less above sea level on the coastal plain and in the Olifants River valley. Furthermore, those in the lower-lying coastal area had more handprints per site than those inland in the mountains.

He concluded that handprints and finger paintings were done more recently than the more conventional rock paintings that underlie them. This was confirmed by the radiocarbon dating of a black finger painting in the Cederberg to 500 years ago. He then reasoned that, as the Khoekhoen herders were relatively recent immigrants to the south-western Cape about 2000 years ago, they were most likely to have been responsible for handprints and finger paintings. But does the distribution of paintings of sheep coincide with the distribution of handprints and finger paintings?

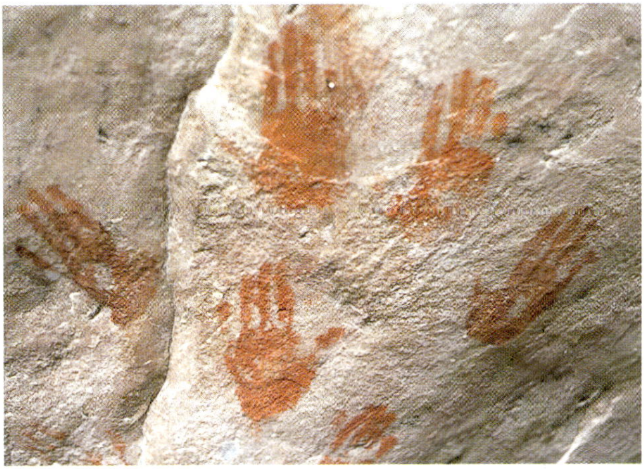

Figure 8
Handprints in red ochre.

When Van Rijssen plotted the distribution of paintings of sheep in the south-western Cape, he found that not only are sheep paintings quite rare – they were found at only 12 out of a total of over 2 000 sites – but they occur almost exclusively in the mountains. As the Khoekhoen kept their sheep mostly on the coastal plain according to archaeological and written records, there seems to be little connection between sheep paintings, handprints and finger paintings. The style of sheep paintings is another interesting anomaly. Bill van Rijssen, Royden Yates, Tony Manhire and John Parkington have all pointed out that the sheep are painted in the same representational way as game animals, using the same controlled method with similar attention to detail. There is nothing to link them technically with the crude finger paintings. There are grounds, then, for believing that sheep paintings were done by the hunter-gatherer San rather than by the immigrant Khoekhoen.

The absence of paintings of cattle is not easy to explain. Could the San have stopped painting soon after sheep were introduced and before cattle were common in the region? This is a possibility mooted by Yates, Manhire and Parkington who believe that the social upheaval associated with the influx of herders into the region 2000-1600 years ago could have led to the San moving into the mountains. Their contact with herders could also have led to a breakdown in social cohesion and an erosion of the power of the shamans. By the time cattle were introduced into the economy a century or more later, San society may have changed to such an extent that painting was no longer practised in the same way as previously.

Another scenario, suggested by the University of Cape Town archaeologists, is that painting was stimulated at times when shamans tried to control difficult situations for the benefit of their society, as for example in times of social upheaval. If this were the case, they argue, most of the paintings in the Cederberg were probably done in response to the initial arrival of herders when the San felt threatened and retreated to the mountains. It would not, however, explain the lack of sheep paintings on the coastal plain nor the absence of paintings of cattle. And one would have expected more sheep paintings, particularly ones associated with trance images.

The difficulty of working out meaning and authorship of the paintings simply by looking at them and recording them is obvious. It is clear, too, that without the written records of the experiences of the /Xam and the Kalahari Bushmen by people from Europe and the Americas, it would have remained impossible to analyse the rock art of southern Africa with any accuracy. It would be just as difficult for a San person to interpret the paintings in a medieval church in Europe without the aid of a Bible. When looking at any religious art we have to come to terms with the fact that although it may look realistic and we can identify particular images as people, sheep, elephant or eland, the art carries deep symbolic and metaphoric meanings that cannot be understood without some clues from the practitioners of that religion. The rock art of the Cederberg is no exception.

A VIEW FROM THE PAINTED RECORD

The view offered in this chapter explores ways in which religious symbols and metaphors are used in the paintings of the Cederberg.

Field surveys of rock paintings in the Cederberg and adjacent river valleys done in the past four decades have made a significant contribution to our knowledge of the distribution of the art and of the range of subject matter and styles. Apart from demonstrating that there are literally thousands of rock paintings in the region, they have confirmed unequivocally that the art uses essentially similar symbols and metaphors to those in rock paintings and engravings in the rest of South Africa.

As a result of these surveys one can cite numerous statistics. For example, paintings of people outnumber animals by between 2:1 and 4:1; gender is clearly indicated in less than half of the human figures, but men are five times more likely to be depicted clearly than women; the average number of people in group scenes is about 15; plants are very rarely illustrated; the eland is the most common animal; and antelope usually account for between 40 and 50% of all the animals depicted.

Other observations we can make relate to San lifestyle and material culture: carrying-bags made of animal skins were popular; some people wore long karosses; bows and arrows were used by men and digging sticks with stone weights were used mainly by women; some people wore strings of beads around the head, neck, legs and arms; and dancing was the most commonly depicted group activity.

Such statistics are interesting, but it is in details of the paintings that most insights are to be found. These details are not easy to spot if you don't know what to look for, particularly if the paintings are faded. You can be led astray by pictures which appear to be real but are not. The reward is in taking time to look closely.

When you come to a painted site you can increase your enjoyment of the experience several fold if you sit quietly and try to work out what it is you are seeing. Read the do's and don'ts on page 57 and tell your children what to do or they may damage the paintings inadvertently.

You can get close to the paintings if this will help you to see more, but never touch them or wet them. Be sure, too, that you do not brush against painted surfaces with your clothing or rucksack and do not to stir up dust.

Never write your name or anything else on rock shelter walls.

Be patient: you will not expect to know everything about the history of South African art by looking at paintings of mountains by Tinus de Jongh, or by counting the number of angels in a painting of the nativity, so take the paintings one at a time. You need to build up some experience to improve your powers of observation and to apply the basic principles of the San belief system to what you see.

Remember, too, that interpreting San rock paintings is not like bird watching or botany, so don't feel frustrated or disappointed if you cannot identify everything. Knowing something about San ethnography will help you to understand that the context is essentially a religious one that was immensely important to the artist. Some of the metaphors the painter used will therefore be explicable, but others are unique or idiosyncratic and cannot be deciphered after such a long time has elapsed. An element of mystery will always remain.

Looking

- On first approaching a rock shelter, check whether paintings are visible. They may be tucked away, but most are there for everyone to see. Maybe there are paintings on the ceiling, or in a crack, or near the ground. Some may be obscured by deposits of natural salts where rain water has dripped and others may be visible only when the rock face is in shadow.
- For many people it is the ambience of the site that gives them greatest pleasure. The view is often spectacular, or it may just be a cool haven from the hot summer sun. Don't forget that the San appreciated these

qualities too and part of the purpose of painting was to mark places in the landscape where the artist may have had a revelationary religious experience that changed his or her life.

- ❐ Get a general idea of the range of images. How many different kinds of human figures can you see? Are the people large or small? Male, female or indeterminate? Are there handprints, dots, zigzags or other patterns? What animals are depicted? Are they mostly antelope, or can you also see a hunting dog, an elephant or lion? You may even see birds or fish if you are lucky. If you think you see a dinosaur, though, you may be confused by the scale!
- ❐ Start taking a closer look. Counting images helps you to search the rock face more thoroughly, so do a rough count of handprints or other images that may be common. Do clearly male figures outnumber females or are they too unspecific? Are the handprints and dots superimposed on top of other paintings? Are the animals easily identifiable to species or have they been transformed? Are there lines joining the figures or encircling them?
- ❐ If you want to start an absorbing hobby, make up a recording sheet like the one at the back of this book. Fill in a sheet for each site you visit and start accumulating some statistics. The South African Museum has a recording centre that would be interested in receiving copies of your records, so contact them and make sure you will be gathering the kind of information that will be useful to the museum.
- ❐ Select a group of figures and look for even more detail. What features can you see that are non-realistic? Let us take a painting that was traced by Stephen Townley Bassett from a site in the Cederberg Wilderness Area as an example (*Figure 9, next page*).

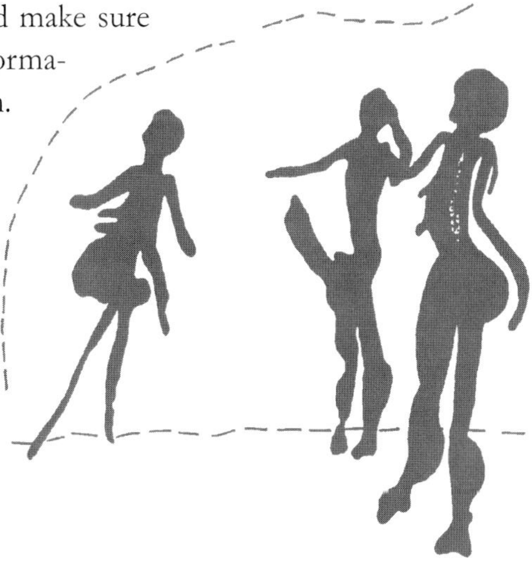

Analysing

At first glance the painting is of a group of 13 or 14 people in a line, all facing in the same direction. Two are badly faded and the one on the far left is indistinct. Six of the people are clearly male and all but one carries hunting equipment. The fact that we can see that some of them are men because of the presence of a penis is itself interesting because San men did not normally go naked. We are immediately alerted to the fact that this is not a realistic scene from everyday life. Three of the men have tassels on the penis. This, too, is non-representational though it is common in rock art.

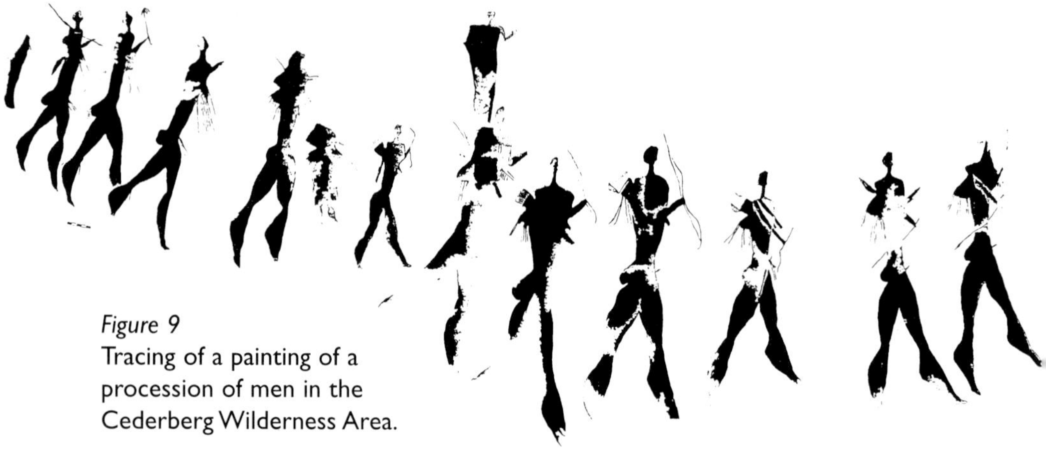

Figure 9
Tracing of a painting of a procession of men in the Cederberg Wilderness Area.

The bodies are elongated and the calves and buttocks are accentuated. While some San may have had a physique like this, it is more likely from what we know of trance experience that the convention of painting people in this way had a ritual connotation. People in a trance-like state report feeling stretched and parts of the body feel enlarged or distorted. Also, the San greatly valued fat which they considered to be highly potent. This may well account for the generously endowed buttocks and calves.

The equipment that the men have carries messages too. The figure second (or third) from the left is holding what looks like a feathery umbrella. It is a fly whisk made from the tail of an animal like a wildebeest. Fly whisks play an important symbolic role in rituals such as the trance dance.

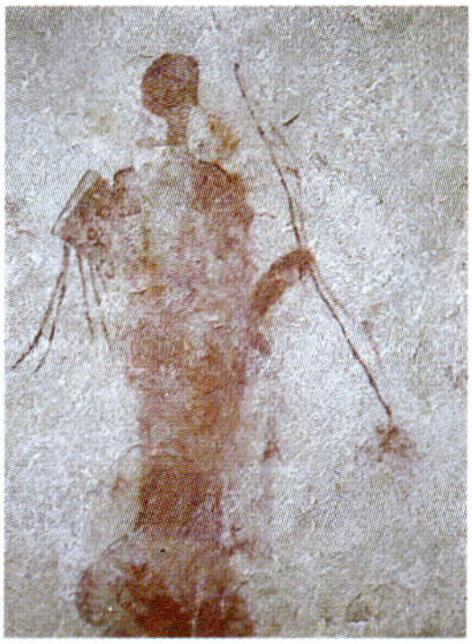

Figure 10
Close-up of a painting of a man carrying a triple-curved bow, from the same panel as Fig 9 and the tracing on p. 4.

The men carry full quivers as well as skin bags with tassels over their shoulders, but some of their bows look oddly bent. They are called triple curved bows (*Figure 10*) and were not known amongst the San in the Western Cape at the time of European contact. Did the San in the Cederberg make bows of this kind hundreds or thousands of years ago? We do not know, but it has been suggested that such paintings show that they did. The figure third from the right carries a bent stick (*Figure 11*). Descriptions of trance hallucinations tell of the transformation of objects such as sticks and bows into odd shapes. Could it be that the stick was part of an hallucinatory experience?

The fourth (or fifth) figure from the left has an odd-shaped head. It may be an over-interpretation to suggest that the head is lion-like and it is difficult to be sure whether it is or not, but we are reminded that the Bleek and Lloyd records have several references to shamans who became lions while in trance. They would move around the landscape in that form and be recognised as lions by others. They would feel as though they were growing hair on their back. Another shamanic connotation can be seen also in the figure standing above the rest in the middle of the panel. It is wearing a long cloak which reminds us of the comment that the shaman, usually an adult man, wears his cloak more often than other people do because he shivers while in trance. His position set back from the others may indicate his special function.

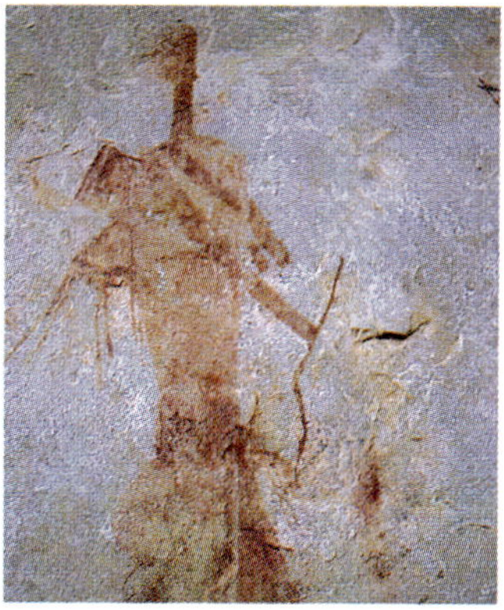

Figure 11
Close-up of a painting of a man carrying a a bent stick from the same panel as Fig 9 and the tracing on p. 22.

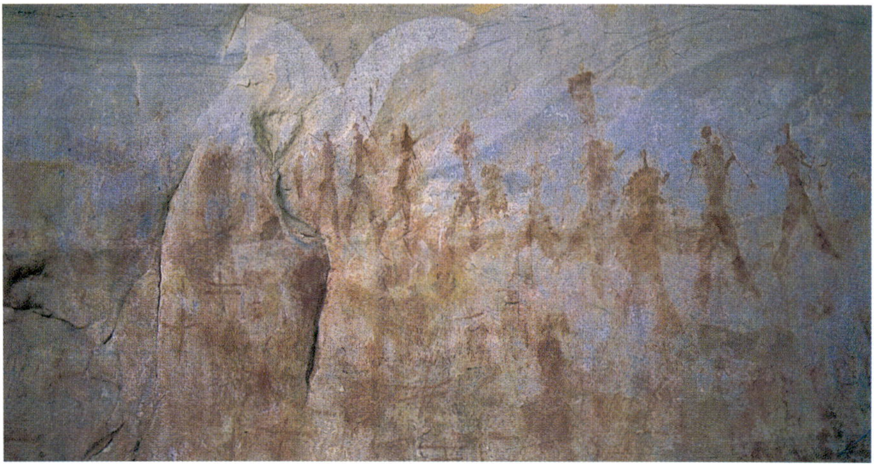

Figure 12
Photo of the same panel as the tracing in Fig 9.

Having looked at the traced figures, look now at the original scene in the colour photograph (*Figure 12*). Here you can see that the human figures are superimposed on one or more faded white elephant in the background. Superimposition is not uncommon and although we know that it was a deliberate act on the part of the artist to put one image on top of another, it is not easy to work out how much time elapsed between the painting of the images. Bill van Rijssen's observation that handprints consistently overlie all other images has led him to assume that the handprints were done at a later time, but we must also allow that this sequence may have been deliberately created at the same time. The almost ghostly effect of the looming white elephant behind the trance dancing men is particularly powerful and undoubtedly had meaning for the artist and the viewer. The fact that the white paint has faded more than the red is no indication of relative age. At the feet of the fourth and fifth men from the left is a white ostrich that is equally faded (*Figure 13*). Its beak is painted over the foot of the fifth man. There were therefore two episodes of white painting: the elephant beneath the red human figures and the ostrich that was painted over the human figure. Apart from showing how important details are and how easily they can be overlooked, this exercise of examining a painted panel closely makes one realise how difficult it is to interpret meaning from tracings and photographs. It also emphasises the role that the viewer plays and how his or her prior knowledge can bias the recording process. One is acutely aware that we may select some things and disregard others. The tracing, for example, has selected the clearest images and has left out what was difficult to see. The photograph, on the other hand, is essentially unselective and it is not possible to be certain about what is depicted at this scale of reproduction. Rock art specialists will therefore use both methods of recording. Before drawing conclusions, a long time must be spent at the rock face to make some decisions about what the artist intended. You may change your mind several times as pieces of the puzzle begin falling into place.

By now the reader will be asking impatiently, "Well, what does the scene mean?"

Thirty years ago we would have confidently called it a 'hunting scene' and may even have suggested that the men were hunting elephant. In the early 1990s, scores of similar scenes in the Western Cape and elsewhere, have been recorded. A much broader understanding of San beliefs and customs, and the knowledge that many of the images are symbols and metaphors rather than depictions of reality, help to suggest something different. We would also be a lot less dogmatic about the meaning. Rather than giving specific explanations for individual paintings, we can point to principles behind the artistic tradition that may help to understand some of the decisions that the artists made.

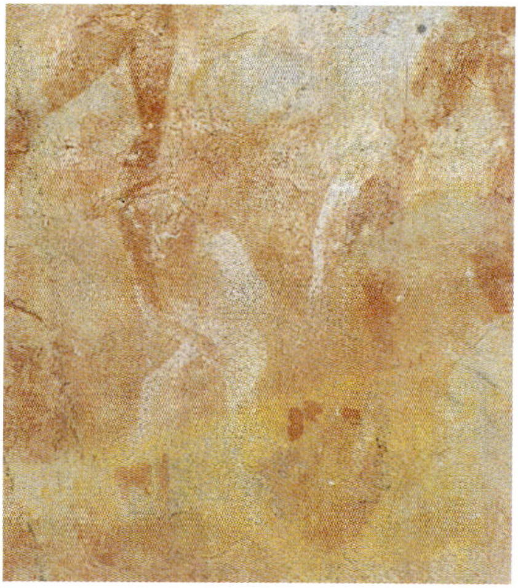

Figure 13

Close-up of a portion of the panel in Fig 9 and Fig 12 showing a white ostrich painted over the leg of one of the men.

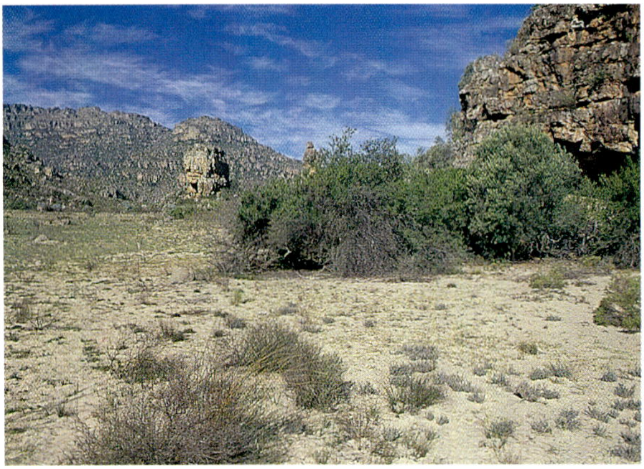

Figure 14
The setting of the site with the painted panel in Figs 9 – 13.

Having accepted that this is a religious art and also that the paintings are mostly non-representational and not 'photographs' of real life, we can see that the men are not in fact hunting. They are dressed without pubic coverings, they are unnaturally elongated, they carry several items normally used in ceremonial dances, and although their hunting equipment is prominently displayed, it is not ready for the kill. A better explanation, particularly in view of the presence of the karossed figure in the background who would symbolise a shaman or initiated man, is a suggestion from John Parkington and his colleagues. This is that such panels illustrate young men in the process of being initiated as adults.

Initiates were associated with animals that had powerful connotations in the San belief system and this could account for the white elephants and the ostrich. This interpretation is based on the knowledge that initiation ceremonies were performed by nineteenth and twentieth century San groups together with ritual dancing and would have involved trancing and altered states of consciousness. The superimposition of people on top of elephants could therefore have been 'seen' by the artist amongst the group during the ceremony. The vision would have been recorded in paint after the event to illustrate the powerful experience and to inspire those who saw it later. The initiation may have occurred at the rock shelter where the painting was done, or on the flat ground outside it (*Figure 14*). The painting enhanced the power of that place and the influence it had on the lives of the initiates.

Deciphering details

Some of the most convincing evidence for the religious nature of the rock art of the Cederberg can be seen in details such as the postures of people, the conventions used for depicting both people and animals, in apparently random lines, and in the symbolic and metaphorical meanings behind realistic images. In the following examples, a few of these details are explored. They provide only a brief introduction. If you would like to know more you will find considerable enjoyment in the books in the reading list at the end of this guide.

Group scene

In the painting traced in *Figure 15*, another kind of group scene is depicted. This time, although all the people on the left are clearly men, they carry no hunting equipment. As with the first panel described above, there are shadowy karossed figures standing in the background. On the left-hand side the men are standing on a double line, but it changes direction several times on the right. The people on the right have assumed strange postures, yet all are still connected to the double line.

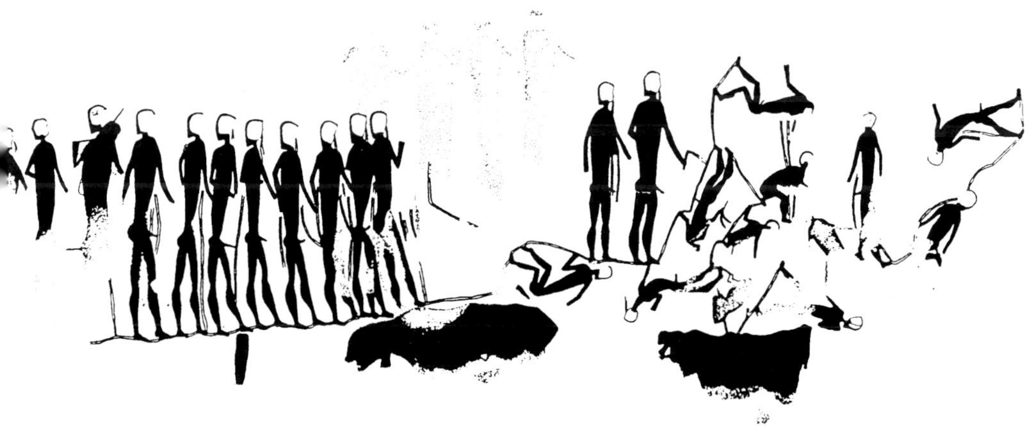

Figure 15
A group of people joined by a red line.

The clues that indicate that this is a trance dance have been well substantiated by studies of twentieth century San in Botswana and Namibia. In a fascinating book called *Boiling energy*, Richard Katz, a psychologist and educationist at the Harvard Medical School, describes the healing or trance dances of the !Kung San. Healers, encouraged by others in the group who also dance, clap and sing, will dance around the fire through the night and their feet will make a well defined path in the sand (depicted by the double line in the painting). They will hyperventilate, sweat and sometimes bleed from the nose (nasal blood is indicated by red lines from the faces of most of the men standing on the left of the panel). As they enter trance they may double up as the diaphragm contracts (see the figure bending from the waist in the middle of the group on the right). The person will then collapse into a deep trance, assuming postures like those of the prostrate figures connected to the line on the right.

When entering this stage of deep trance the San say that they 'die' and feel as though their spirit leaves their body. In this state they may feel as though they are flying through the air or swimming under water or even travelling underground. That is why, in some paintings, healers are shown associated with fish or birds. During the trance dance, those in the group who are healers will take sweat from their body and blood from their nose and put it on to sick people who wish to be healed. They will draw the sickness out of the person with their hands and the sickness will travel through the body of the healer and exit through the back of the neck or head. The line coming out of the head of the figure on the far right may illustrate the path of this power.

The two patches of red paint at the bottom of this tracing are difficult to decipher with certainty, but as the double line enters each one and comes out again, they must be part of the composition. They may be the remains of faded paintings of animals, possibly eland. Eland were regarded as being sources of great potency. They were frequently painted with a red torso and yellow and white legs, neck and head. As the white and yellow paint does not last as well as the red, often only the red torso remains.

Lines

The next painting (*Figure 16*) has a group of four seated figures. There are two or three others to the left of the traced part of the panel that are less distinct. The four seated people are connected by a meandering zigzag line that joins the heads of three of them and intersects a red line coming from the head of the fourth. The second person from the right has a white line coming from the mouth or nose. This is not as easy to interpret as the line on which the people were standing in the previous example. Having seen many similar lines in paintings throughout South Africa, David Lewis-Williams has suggested that they represent lines of potency or magic force. They illustrate the feeling of supernatural 'electricity' or power that the healers interviewed by Richard Katz reported receiving from God during trance.

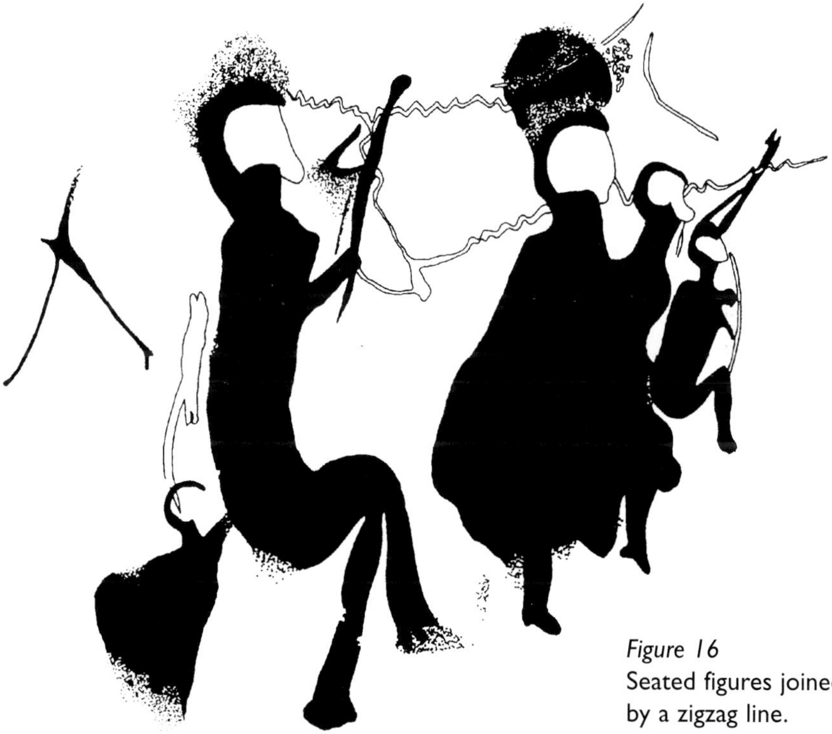

Figure 16
Seated figures joined by a zigzag line.
Scale in cm

Not all paintings show these features so clearly. Sometimes the only indication of trance is a person bending forward (*Figure 17*), or a small group of dancing and clapping women (*Figure 18*), or a group of elongated people. Equally intriguing are paintings of very tiny people, often done with such fine detail that they are impossible to trace with accuracy. This, too, could be an indication of an altered state of consciousness. Just as people in trance or in a dream may feel elongated or distorted, they may also feel as though they are shrinking. This feeling is common in dreams and trance-like states. For example, when Alice, in her dream, follows the rabbit underground in Lewis Carroll's story of *Alice in Wonderland*, she drinks from a bottle and grows very tall, and then eats some cake and becomes very small.

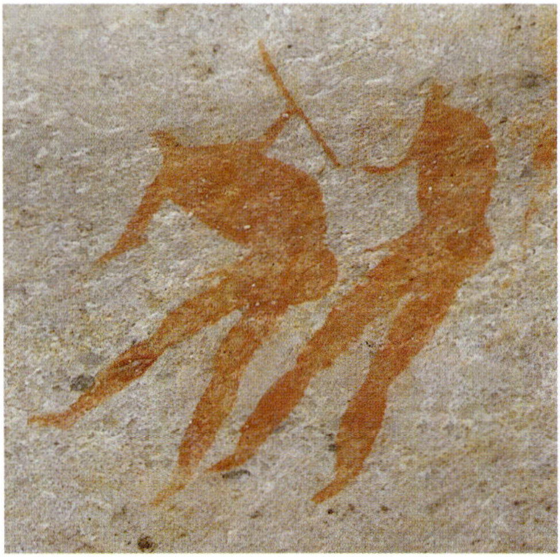

Figure 17
Human figure bent at the waist.

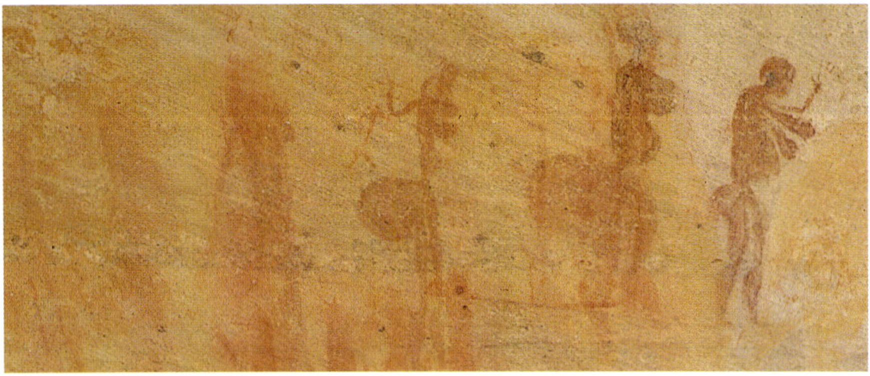

Figure 18
Clapping and dancing women.

Elephant

Paintings of animals, with great care given to detail and apparent realism, can be equally challenging to interpret. The well-known panel with large, clear paintings of elephants alongside two groups of people in procession near the so-called Stadsaal in the Cederberg, is but one example (*Figure 19*). Elephants have a lot of body fat which is a source of potency for the San. Ju/'hoan Bushmen in Namibia told Megan Biesele in the 1970s that some people will not eat elephant meat because it is said to be like that of people. In her book *Women like Meat*, she recalls that they then drew further comparisons between physical characteristics of elephants and people (particularly women) to show how closely the two are connected. Of special interest is the fact that elephants are said to dance like people. Comparisons like these are significant because they suggest that rock paintings of elephants are metaphors for shamans and the things that shamans do. In the case of the Stadsaal painting, the two rows of dancing people are mirrored in the two rows of elephants and could be illustrating the way in which trance dancers 'become' animals they revere and from which they draw power.

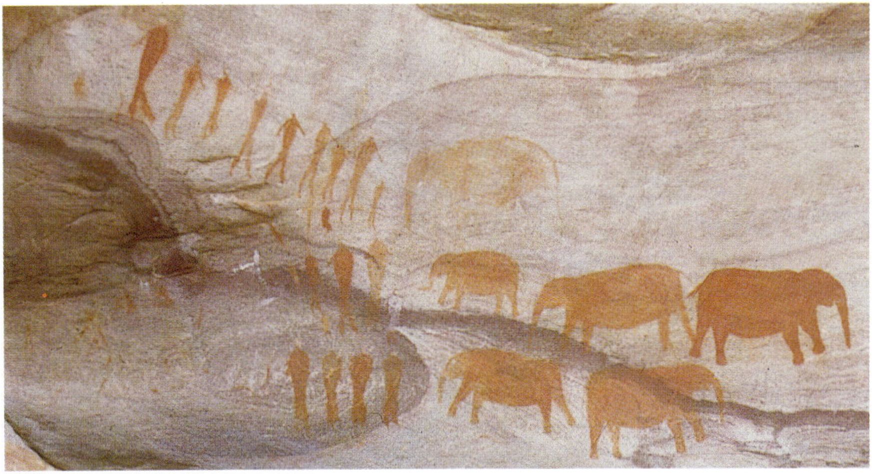

Figure 19
Elephants at a rock shelter near the Stadsaal.

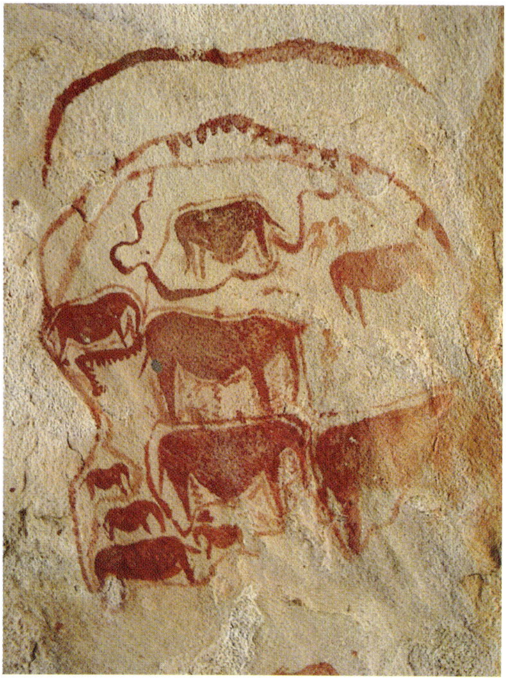

Figure 20
Elephants surrounded by lines.

One of the important services offered by San shamans was rain making. A /Xam man named Dia!kwain from the Calvinia district who was interviewed by Bleek and Lloyd in the 1870s explained how a rain maker worked. He would enter into a trance and his spirit would leave his body and capture the rain animal in a water pit. To tame it, young girls would sprinkle a sweet-smelling herb called buchu on the water. He would lead the rain animal across the veld and kill it. It would rain where the blood and milk of the rain animal fell. The rain animal was depicted as large and bulky and when shown a copy of a rock painting from the Eastern Cape, Dia!kwain identified an amorphous hippo-like creature surrounded by wavy lines as a rain animal.

A similar painting from the Cederberg, *Figure 20*, shows elephants within wavy lines hinting that they, too, could have been used in rain making. One explanation of the significance of the wavy lines around the elephants is that they represent the aura seen around visions during trance. A second suggestion is that they represent clouds. A third possibility is that they are another example of lines of potency or magic force. Whatever the motivation of the artist, the lines reinforce the non-reality of the paintings. They place the painting firmly in the realm of visions that are merged with patterns of light – sometimes called entoptics – seen during trance.

Eland

The San deity, /Kaggen, was a trickster and could take many forms. He often took the form of the Mantis and this led to the belief amongst Europeans that the San 'worshipped' the Mantis. This perception is mirrored in the Afrikaans name for the praying mantis: Hotnotsgod or 'Hottentot God'. /Kaggen is not shown realistically in the rock art, but does appear symbolically. People, for example, are sometimes painted with a mantis-shaped head; human or animal limbs are sometimes angled in the same way as those of the mantis; and items and animals associated with /Kaggen and his powers are included in many paintings.

The eland was the first animal that /Kaggen created and it remained his favourite. It is the most commonly depicted antelope in both rock paintings and rock engravings throughout southern Africa. In the Cederberg, as elsewhere, it is also the most carefully painted and takes many forms. *Figure 21* shows a beautifully shaded polychrome painting of a herd of eland cows. *Figure 22* (*next page*) is a good example of a transformation of a person to an eland: it appears to be an ordinary eland, but the back legs are human legs.

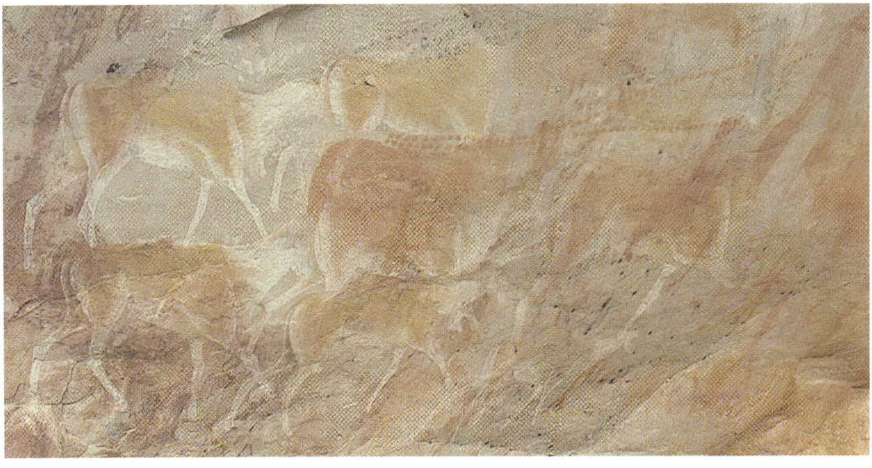

Figure 21
A group of eland painted in shaded polychrome.

In the Drakensberg, where rock paintings often show more detail than those in the Western Cape, David Lewis-Williams has document-ed a number of clear examples of eland therianthropes. A the-rianthrope combines human and animal characteristics, rather like the centaur in Greek mythology. He has concluded that eland, and particularly paintings that depict dying eland, are a metaphor for the shaman in trance. When an eland is dying it does a number of things that a shaman does when he 'dies' or enters trance. It staggers, its head falls forward, it bleeds from the nose or mouth, its hair stands upright along its back and it sweats profusely. The very presence of a painting of an eland, even though the painting may not show bleeding from the nose or hair standing upright along its back, may be a metaphor for a trancing shaman and not simply a painting of an eland. This concept is similar to that of the lamb in Christian thought. The lamb was the animal traditionally used for sacrifices to God and also represents the 'lamb of God' or the sacrifice that Christ made at the crucifixion. The lamb is therefore a metaphor for Christ.

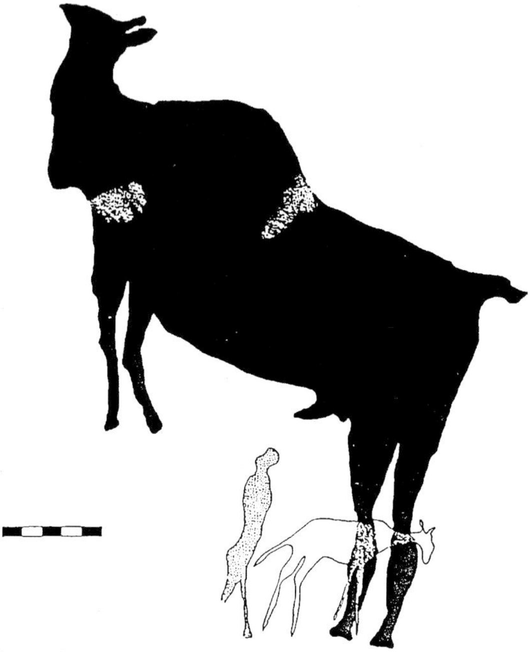

Figure 22
An eland with human hind legs. Scale in cm.

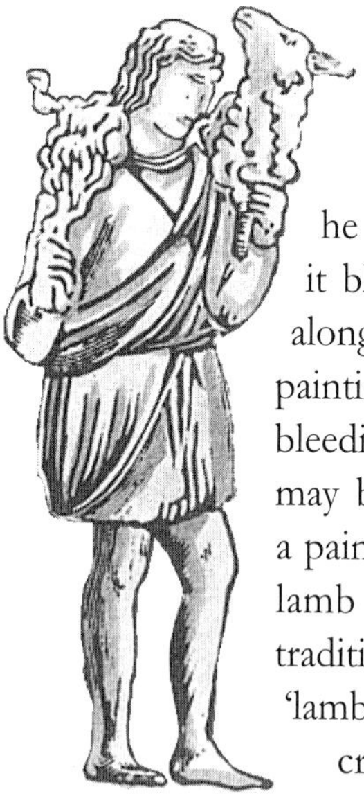

Sheep

We have discussed at length the implications of the introduction of domesticated animals for the history of the San in the Western Cape, but what can be said about paintings of sheep? There is an interesting folktale recorded by Bleek and Lloyd and published in 1924 by Dorothea Bleek called "The Mantis takes away the Ticks' Sheep". The Ticks are said to be metaphors for the Korana, the Khoekhoe herders who were living along the Orange River and in Bushmanland alongside the /Xam in the eighteenth and nineteenth centuries. /Kaggen in the form of a Mantis goes to the Ticks' house and when they see him coming they hide in the wool of the sheep. While he is sitting at their fire, they fall off the sheep one by one and attack him, holding down his kaross. He has to slip out of the kaross to get away, but later calls to his kaross, his hartebeest-skin bag, his stick and his quiver to follow him and they all fly away.

Back home, the Ichneumon (mongoose) said: "You went to the house to which people do not go ... for those people are wont to beat a man to death because of those sheep." That night the Mantis dreams that all the Ticks' houses and their sheep rise up and come to his, the Mantis's, house. When he wakes in the morning they are there and his family and friends rejoice in their good fortune but are also uneasy. When the Dassie asks /Kaggen why he took the sheep, he answers "It seemed right to me, because these people attacked me". And he explains to the Ichneumon "Do you not see why I thought it right? These people did bad deeds to me, ... I wish that those people may themselves see what I can do and recognise it. For they would not give me food that I might return".

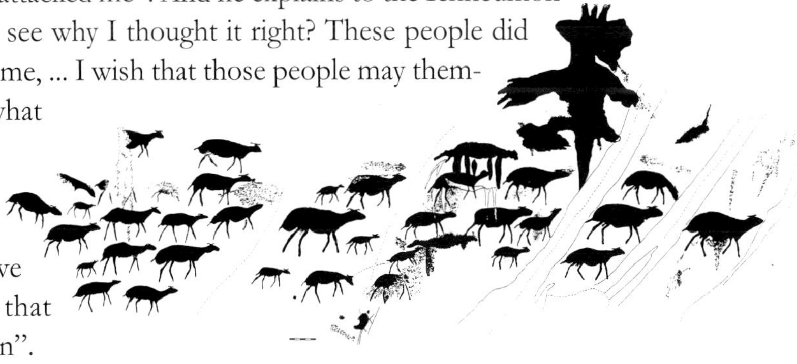

The tale illustrates a number of concepts. First is the matter of ownership and sharing. /Kaggen speaks for the /Xam belief that food should be shared and that polite people do not attack a visitor at their home, nor do they keep food only for themselves. He steals the sheep to teach the Ticks a lesson: that they should share the sheep. This reflects a deep-seated resentment amongst the /Xam against Khoekhoen that may have been common to other hunter-gatherers too. Second are the references to flying and dreaming, both of which are indicative of trance. /Kaggen, the medicine man or shaman, is able to manipulate a situation by going into a trance or dream and turning it to his advantage. Third, the concept that a bag or kaross will retain some of the power and characteristics of the animal from which the skin came is common amongst the San. It suggests that a painting of a bag can also be a metaphor for the animal whose skin it was. Bags are often painted in the Cederberg and an example is shown in *Figure 23*.

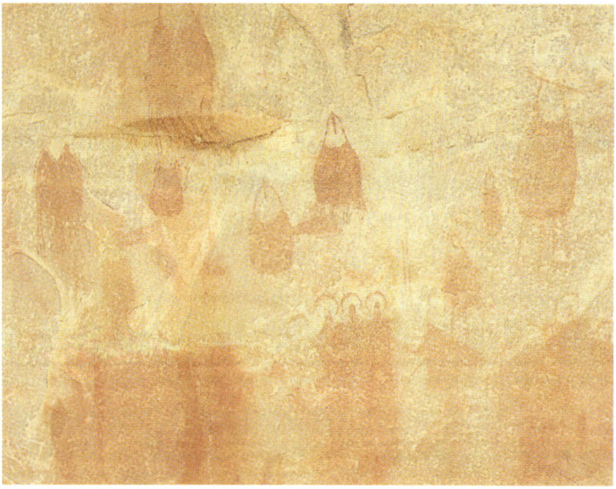

Figure 23
Painting of bags, some of which are hanging on pegs.

Such a tale is helpful in drawing meaning from a painting such as the one illustrated in the tracing on p. 51. It may well represent the dream or trance of a shaman who 'captures' sheep from the Khoekhoen to manipulate a situation of conflict for the benefit of his people. That this could be the case is strengthened by the presence of a small figure in the centre of the panel near the bottom. Is this perhaps the Mantis in disguise?

European images

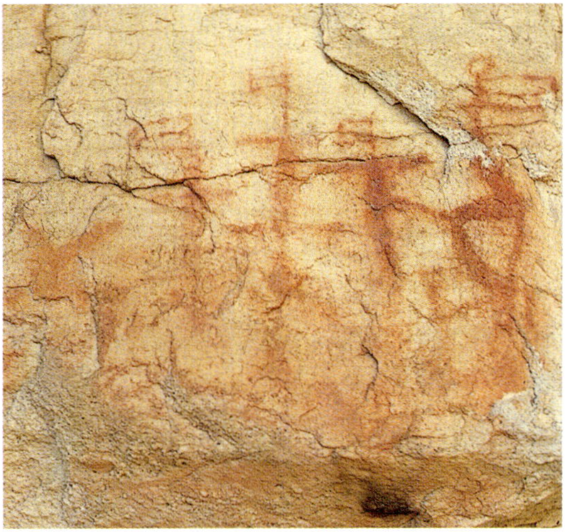

Figure 24
Painting of a sailing ship with flags.

The last examples of rock paintings illustrate the final chapter of the history of San artists in the Western Cape by depicting images of European origin. One of the most enigmatic is a finger painting of a sailing ship in the mountains east of Porterville (*Figure 24*). Unfortunately it is now somewhat faded and is deteriorating rapidly as it is painted on very friable rock and visitors have relentlessly wetted and touched it. The flags face in different directions indicating that the artist was probably not a sailor, but must either have been at the coast and seen a sailing ship, or must have been told about it by someone else.

The motivation for the painting is unknown. Although we cannot be certain that it was done by a Khoisan person, the suggestion that finger paintings were done relatively recently is bolstered by the fact that this one depicts a ship. We could hazard a guess that, if the painting was done by a shaman, the artist was trying to exert some kind of control on ships and their sailors by calling up the image in a trance, but there are no other clues in the vicinity to help resolve the question or identify the artist. Just below the painting of the ship someone has illegally removed a slab of rock that probably had a painting on it.

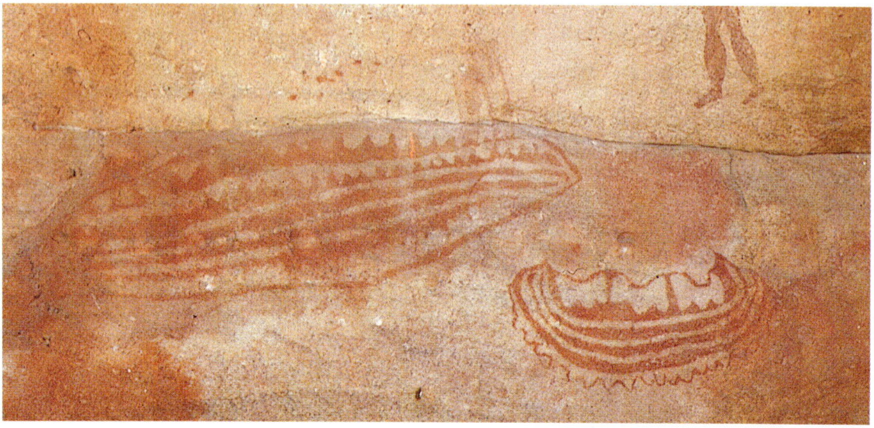

Figure 25
An entoptic painting assumed by some to be a ship (*lower right*).

The painting at the lower right hand side of *Figure 25* has also been called a ship, but with the knowledge we now have of the form that trance visions may take, it is much more likely to be purely visionary. Although generally 'boat-shaped' it bears no resemblance to any known sea-going vessel, and indeed it is doubtful that such a vessel would ever have completed the journey from Europe (or indeed from any other far-off place) to the Western Cape. When seen next to the longer shape to the left, its origin as an entoptic vision is even more obvious.

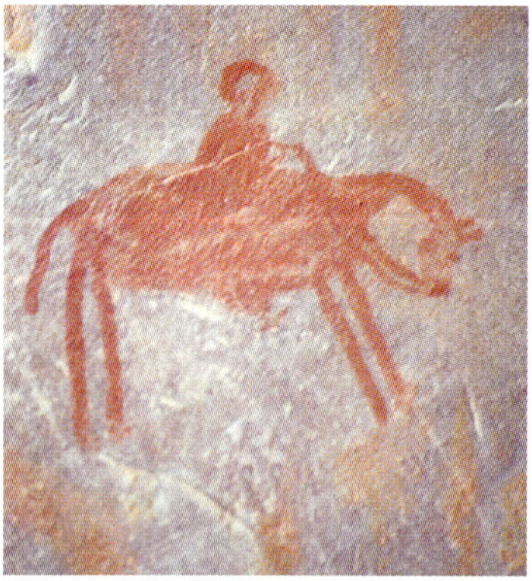

Figure 26
Painting of a horseman.

The mounted horseman in *Figure 26* must post-date the 1650s when the Dutch imported the first horses into South Africa. Seen in isolation it may seem simply to be a picture of a man on a horse. It is in fact part of a larger panel (*Figure 27, next page*) that includes 'imaginary' animals as well as an entoptic pattern, both of which indicate that it, too, is trance-related.

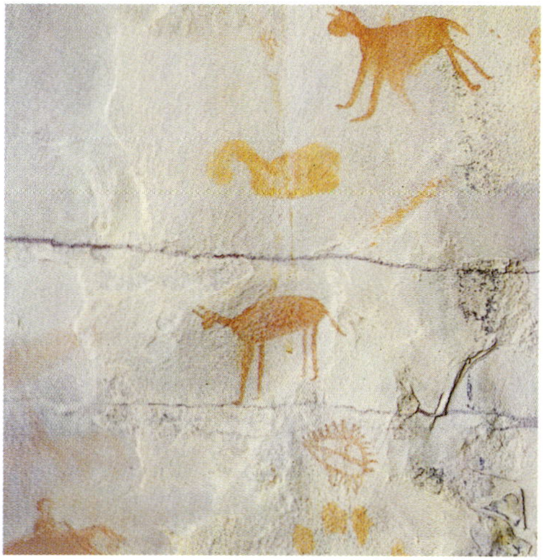

Figure 27
Panel of finger paintings. The horseman in Fig 26 is at bottom left.

Conclusions

These few examples will not enable you to decipher all the rock paintings you may see in the Cederberg. This would be an impossible task. Not only are we faced with a large number of paintings that cannot be dated, but also with the work of individual artists, each of whom painted their own personal experiences or those of their contemporaries. The effect of such personal variations in rock art has been recognised in the Drakensberg by Thomas Dowson but has not yet been studied in the Western Cape. We know, too, that our ethnographic record is limited and although it has provided vital clues, there is much we may never know. The descriptions will, however, give you an insight into the depth of meaning that the paintings contain. We have focused here on the kinds of images and transformations that are induced by trance experience, but there are undoubtedly other such experiences and beliefs that influenced the art as well. Perhaps you will be inspired to read further, especially about the twentieth century San.

Understanding the concepts outlined in this book will have made it clear that rock paintings are not simplistic daubings by child-like primitive people. They are instead a remarkably resilient religious art form that demonstrates more eloquently than any written words the full power and sophistication of the San belief system that lasted for thousands of years in southern Africa. Rock art is one of the oldest forms of historical record and deserves to be recognised as a vital part of our heritage.

A VIEW OF THE FUTURE: CONSERVATION OF ROCK PAINTINGS

Rock paintings in the Cederberg are highly vulnerable to damage caused by people. About 10% of the sites in the Cederberg Wilderness Area have graffiti on or near to the paintings. Graffiti date back to the seventeenth century (*Figure 28*) and are still damaging rock art today (*Figure 29*). Damage is done both deliberately and accidentally. When you visit a site with rock art, be aware that the paintings are fragile and behave as you would in a place of worship such as a church or a mosque, or in a place where precious things are displayed, such as an art gallery, museum or antique shop.

You may think that by touching the paintings just once you cannot do any damage, but research in many parts of the world has proven that rock paintings at sites that are visited often will fade much more quickly than those at sites that are seldom visited. This is because there is a cumulative effect from all those who think it will not matter if they touch the paintings as long as no-one else does.

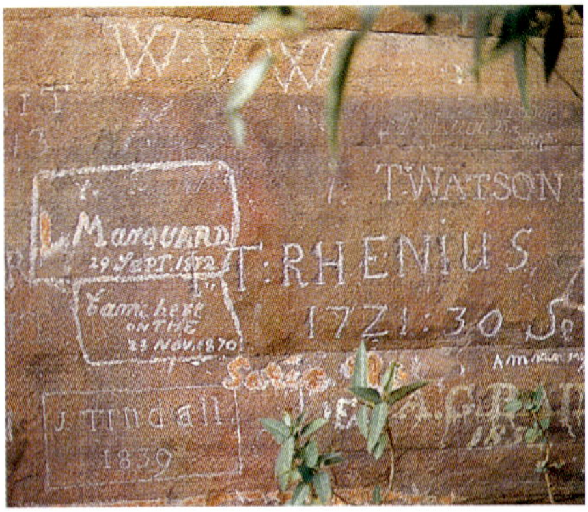

Figure 28
Early graffiti at the Heerenlogement.

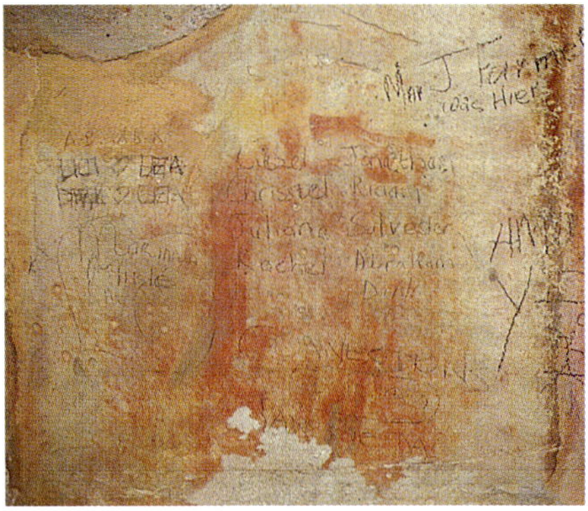

Figure 29
Recent graffiti at Wiedou.

You can make a positive contribution towards conserving rock paintings for your children and for their children if you do the following:

- ❒ Keep your hands to yourself and do not touch the paintings. Even the smallest amount of moisture on your fingers will cause damaging salts to accumulate at the rock surface. They will form a film and cover the paint, or the salt crystals will expand with the moisture and cause small particles of paint and rock to flake off.
- ❒ Keep water away from painted surfaces and don't even think of putting it or any other substance on the paintings. Salts will be drawn to the surface of the rock where they expand and destroy the paint.
- ❒ Keep fires outside painted rock shelters. The soot and moisture from cooking will damage the paintings irreparably.
- ❒ Be careful that your rucksack, backpack, camera bag or clothing will not brush against painted surfaces as this wears away the particles of rock and the paint that is attached to them.
- ❒ Walk slowly and carefully when you are in a painted rock shelter so that you do not stir up dust. The fine particles stick to the painted surfaces where they become fixed by moisture in the rock.

Remind yourself and your friends that it is an offence in terms of the National Monuments Act (Act No. 28 of 1969) to destroy, damage or alter rock paintings or to remove them from their original site or export them from the Republic without a permit from the National Monuments Council.

- ❒ If convicted of an offence in terms of the Act, the penalty is a fine of up to R10 000 or two years' imprisonment, or both.
- ❒ If you see anyone damaging rock paintings, obtain information about their identity and report the matter to the police immediately.
- ❒ If you would like to be involved in recording rock art sites, you can obtain copies of the South African Museum's site recording form from the Museum's Department of Archaeology (address on page 59).

ROCK PAINTING SITES OPEN TO THE PUBLIC

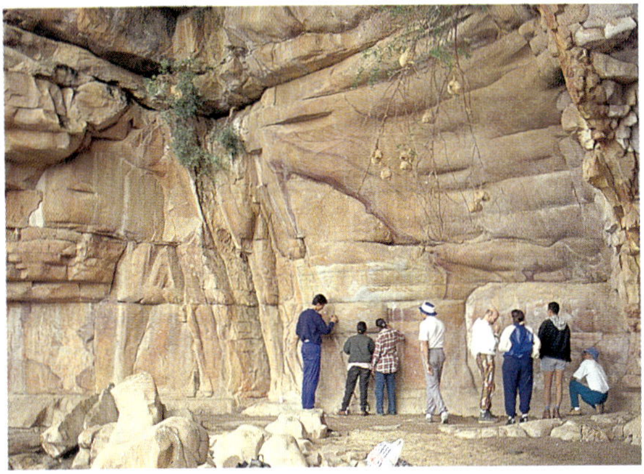

Figure 30
A team from the National Monuments Council removing graffiti at Kagga Kamma.

The policy of Western Cape Nature Conservation with regard to the wilderness areas in their care is not to advertise their attractions, but to allow visitors to discover them for themselves.

For this reason we have not identified the location of sites in the wilderness areas, but there are a few privately owned properties in the Cederberg where rock painting sites are open to the public. If you would like to visit them, please do so. The sites are identified on the map on page 11.

Site	**Contact person**	**Telephone**
The Baths, Citrusdal	The Manager	(022) 921 3609
Kromrivier, Clanwilliam	Olive Nieuwoudt	(027) 482 2807
Bokwater, Clanwilliam	Stephanie Stone	(027) 482 1940
Travellers Rest, Pakhuis	Haffie Strauss	(027) 482 2629
Bushmanskloof, Pakhuis	Mark McAdam	(027) 482 2627
	Reservations	(021) 797 0990
Kagga Kamma, Ceres	The Manager	(0233) 7 0888
Gifberg, Vanrhynsdorp	Mrs Huisamen	(02727) 91555
Nature Conservation, Citrusdal	Cederberg permits	(022) 921 2289
Wuppertal	Tourist Information	(027) 482 3410

In addition, there are several other places that are open all the time:

- Leipoldt's Grave at the top of Pakhuis Pass east of Clanwilliam has a few faded paintings. This site is very easily accessible.
- The Ceres Nature Reserve at the entrance to the town from the Cape Town side has a small rock shelter with some interesting paintings that are easily accessible, but have been damaged by vandals.
- The Heerenlogement cave near Klawer has a few handprints and faded paintings to the right of the historical graffiti.

Further information can be obtained from:

Department of Archaeology, University of Cape Town, Rondebosch, 7700
Tel. (021) 650 2357

National Monuments Council, P O Box 4637, Cape Town, 8000
Tel. (021) 462 4502

South African Museum, P O Box 61, Cape Town, 8000
Tel. (021) 24 3330

South African Archaeological Society, P O Box 15700, Vlaeberg, 8018
Tel. (021) 24 3330

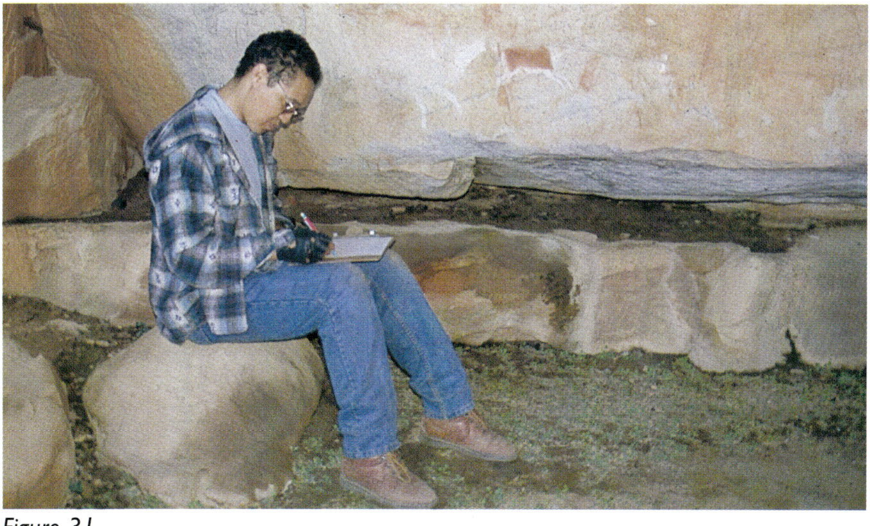

Figure 31
Recording paintings and graffiti before graffiti removal.

ROCK ART SITE RECORD FORM

MAP SHEET: ______________ SITE NO: ______________

LOCAL SITE NAME: ______________

CONTACT PERSON/OWNER: ______________

POSTAL ADDRESS: ______________

RECORDER'S NAME: ______________ PHONE: ______________

ACCOMPANIED BY: ______________

DATE OF VISIT: ______________

Name of nearest access point: ______________

Distance/time from vehicle access point: ______________

Footpath to the site: Yes ❑ No ❑ Part-way ❑

Time/distance from footpath: ______________

Gradient: Low<20° ❑ Moderate 20-40° ❑ Steep 40-90° ❑ Mixed ❑

Terrain: Sandy ❑ Gravel ❑ Stony ❑ Rocky ❑ Low vegetation ❑
Bushy ❑ Thorny ❑ Shaded ❑ Exposed ❑ Difficult ❑ Easy ❑

Type of site: Cave ❑ Overhang ❑ Wall ❑ Boulder ❑ Other ❑

Orientation: N ❑ NE ❑ E ❑ SE ❑ S ❑ SW ❑ W ❑ NW ❑

Size of cave/overhang: Width: ______________ Depth ______________
Height ______________ Area with paintings (sq m) ______________

Natural screening of site: Visibility on approach ______________
Visibility from the site: ______________

Exposure to sunlight: Mornings ❑ Afternoons ❑ All day ❑
Part of site gets no sun ❑ None ❑

Area of frieze affected by sunlight (sq m): ______________

Are painting in danger of disappearing? Yes ❑ No ❑ Maybe ❑

Seepage/drip/lichen/vegetation on rock paintings: Present over <10% ❑
10-50% ❑ >50% ❑ Absent ❑

Vandalism/graffiti: Paint chipped off ❑ Charcoal ❑ Scratches ❑
Smoke ❑ Other ❑

Are graffiti: On paintings ❑ Near paintings ❑ Far from the paintings ❑

Size of area with graffiti: ....

Estimated number of painted images: 1-10 ❑ 10-25 ❑ 50-75 ❑
75-100 ❑ >100 ❑

Clarity of paintings: COLOURS: Bright ❑ Moderate ❑ Faded ❑
EDGES: Clear ❑ Moderate ❑ Fuzzy ❑
DETAIL: Good ❑ Moderate ❑ Poor ❑

Colour of paintings (% total): Red .... Yellow .... White ....
Black .... Bi/Polychrome ....

Subject matter: HUMAN: Male ❑ Female ❑ Indeterminate ❑
Therianthrope ❑ Group scenes ❑

ANIMAL: Antelope ❑ Elephant ❑ Other ❑
Domesticated ❑

HANDPRINTS: Positive ❑ Negative ❑ Patterned ❑
PALETTES: ❑ SMEARED AREAS: ❑ FINGER DOTS: ❑
LINES: ❑ DOTS: ❑

Nature of deposit: Sandy ❑ Ashy ❑ Bedding ❑ None ❑

Artefacts: Present ❑ Absent ❑ OES ❑ Pottery ❑ Charcoal ❑

Access to drinking water: <5 mins ❑ 5-10 mins ❑ 10-20 mins ❑ >20mins ❑

Is site suitable for tourists? Yes ❑ Small groups only ❑ No ❑
Only with guide ❑ Only with noticeboard ❑

Recording: Colour slide ❑ Colour prints ❑ B&W prints ❑
Tracings: All ❑ Selection ❑

Site previously recorded? Yes ❑ No ❑

NOTES: ....

RECOMMENDED READING

Biesele, M. 1993. *Women like meat. The folklore and foraging ideology of the Kalahari Ju/'hoan.* Johannesburg: Witwatersrand University Press.

Dowson, T.A. 1992. *Rock engravings of southern Africa.* Johannesburg: Witwatersrand University Press.

Katz, R.B. 1984. *Boiling energy: community healing among the Kalahari !Kung.* Cambridge, Massachusetts: Harvard University Press.

Lewis-Williams, J.D. 1990. *Discovering southern African rock art.* Cape Town: David Philip.

Lewis-Williams, J.D. & Dowson, T.A. 1989. *Images of power: understanding Bushman rock art.* Johannesburg: Southern Book Publishers.

Lewis-Williams, J.D. & Dowson, T.A. 1992. *Rock paintings of the Natal Drakensberg.* Pietermaritzburg; University of Natal Press.

Vinnicombe, P. 1976. *People of the eland: rock paintings of the Drakensberg Bushmen as a reflection of their life and thought.* Pietermaritzburg: University of Natal Press.

Woodhouse, H.C. 1992. *The Rain and its Creatures.* Johannesburg: William Waterman.

Yates, R., Parkington, J. & Manhire, A. 1990. *Pictures from the past: a history of the interpretation of rock paintings and engravings of southern Africa.* Pietermaritzburg: Centaur.

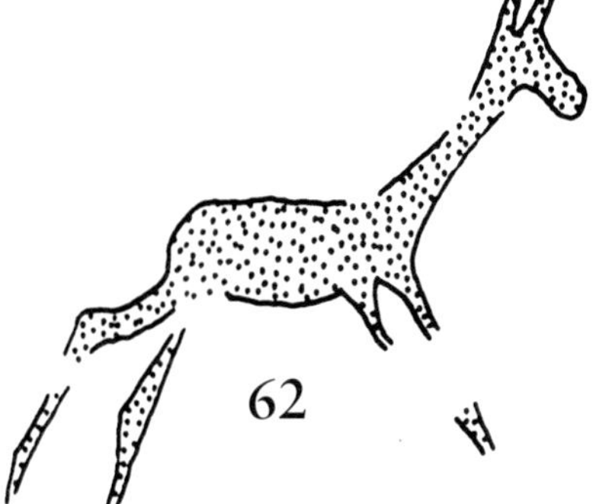